The Shaadi Story

The Shaadi Story

BEHIND THE SCENES OF THE BIG FAT INDIAN WEDDING

Amita Nigam Sahaya

MACMILLAN

First published 2020 by Macmillan
an imprint of Pan Macmillan Publishing India Private Limited
707, Kailash Building,
26, K. G. Marg, New Delhi – 110 001
www.panmacmillan.co.in

Pan Macmillan, The Smithson, 6 Briset Street, London EC1M 5NR
Associated companies throughout the world
www.panmacmillan.com

ISBN 978-93-89109-40-5

1 3 5 7 9 8 6 4 2

Typeset in Minion Pro by R. Ajith Kumar, New Delhi
Printed and bound in India by
Replika Press Pvt. Ltd.

To Gen Next, where love and longing
Celebrate the traditions of yore,
The Wedding – with fast food flavours,
An addictive cocktail
Blessed by social media

And

To the previous generation – your
Indomitable fibre yet tremulous smiles
Cleaved ways through trammelled paths
Kusum and Bimla – beautiful, dutiful mothers
Your stories weave this marital song

CONTENTS

PREFACE

Every book has a memory spurring its writing. Mine is located in a childhood event, whose actual sequence though blurred, had a deep and lasting emotional impact on me. It happened during my aunt's wedding decades ago, and forever since, I have seen every wedding beyond the haze of its partying and merry-making symbolism, for the traditions that are at its core. The power dynamics between the boy-wallahs and girl-wallahs, the spin-offs, the matchmaking, the social equation – what the bride takes with her and what it means to be given away, marriage as a rite of passage in the life of the bride, the groom and also their parents – and finally, the tidal course of the moolah steering the wedding along its grandiose path.

Here is what happened that evening. My aunt's wedding, definitely affected by the regressive values and gender norms prevalent in small-town India of the 1970s, was being conducted. The sonorous sounds of mantras played over the loudspeaker as the priest conducted the ceremony of the bride and the groom going around the sacred fire. In one corner of the wedding ground, the baraatis were helping themselves to mouthwatering food from a buffet of glimmering silver vessels. All seemed to be going well. It was an ideal setting, a picture-postcard version of the greatest show in the life of an average Indian – one's own wedding or that of one's child!

Suddenly and without any warning, the scenario turned into a wedding nightmare. A man, clearly a baraati – wearing a marigold garland and a skewed turban – was shouting, his words though swallowed by the surrounding din, did have a clear sounding accusation, 'How dare you, water poured on my plate … insulted me … I will not tolerate this for even one minute!' There was food spattered on the floor around his feet and some leftover blobs on the plate in his hand. Even without knowing the details of what had actually transpired, one could see that the man was livid and was threatening the most dire consequences in order to teach 'the girls' side' a lesson. Yes, he was going to walk out of the wedding. Alarm bells clanged among the hosts, with the star players within them springing to disaster management. The furious guest had to be somehow appeased and calmed down. While the news travelled around the wedding pandal at lightning speed, the members of the bride's family stood transfixed, some frozen in the act of serving food. For an eternal moment, it seemed that the bridal couple's third phera around the agni was going to be their last, as the baraat chorused their intent of walking away from the wedding. That would have ended the marriage even before it had begun. The stalemate had the ominous ring of a predator's preparatory steps before he leaps for the jugular. But before that fatal leap my grandfather rushed into the breach – the father of the bride, his youthful physique bent by the catastrophe that stared him in the face. Without a moment's hesitation he whipped off the turban from his head, a symbol of masculine pride and honour, and placed it at the furious baraati's feet – an act of sheer supplication, a plea for forgiveness, condensed into that single fluid movement. The baraati softened at the gesture and the day was saved. The mantras resumed and shehnai sounds filled the air once again.

This scene, though a curtain-raiser, showcases several tropes that define the Indian wedding – the celebratory, the problematic and their interstices. This book focuses on several of these tropes through the lens of the typical North Indian wedding, or the Big Fat Indian Wedding as the sub-title suggests, through its seven chapters strung together like the *saptapadi*, or rounds of the sacred fire and the accompanying vows.[1] Each chapter explores and examines a particular aspect of the Indian wedding. The *saptapadi* is variously adapted by local communities across most forms of Hindu weddings over many geographical regions – a pan-Indian imagery representing the wedding ceremony. The practice is prevalent in the northern parts of the country such as the states of Uttar Pradesh, Rajasthan, Punjab, Bihar and Madhya Pradesh, and remains central to weddings in Bengal and Orissa. Moving towards the south of the country, Tamil weddings too celebrate *saptapadi* following the *homam*, as do Kannadiga and Telugu weddings.

I am taking considerable liberties in conflating the Hindu wedding practices and customs as 'Indian'. I seek the readers' generosity to help encompass a vastness of scale that would challenge even encyclopedic compilations. While India's diversity of religions, castes and communities, the minutiae of rituals and regional customs, myriad belief systems and forms of worship inject a definition-defying richness to the idea of Indianness, it is impossible to fit it all into a box. For me to attempt encompassing this civilizational magnitude in this book, would be far beyond its reach or scope. And so, we employ particular images to convey a larger picture. References and anecdotes, vignettes of weddings, certain rituals and thought processes, which are present in the north Indian Hindu milieu, also have some commonality across state boundaries. It's a picture that a wider audience relates to, a popular image of the Indian wedding that does represent a shared sensibility and idiom, though specific rituals and customs may vary across regional boundaries and cultures.

While some sociologists[2] opine that small sample sizes must not generalize a people, other equally eminent ones[3,4] prefer examining diversities through certain universal practices 'where they project the similarity in principles and the underlying identity in the essentials of the structure'. I follow the latter argument here, focussing on a general Indianness of sensibility, thought processes, social and cultural structures, fears and superstitions, which together form the essence of the Indian social fabric and aid our understanding of a key event – the wedding.

We now come to contemporary times. Yes, the times have changed. The humble family-style Indian wedding has metamorphosed into a big, fat, movie-like celebration, embracing the ambitious appetite of a 'new' India. Weddings have become bigger, grander and a designer's spectacle, with the bride and the groom enacting a dreamy fantasy of ultimate, unstoppable love in the best of the Bollywoodian tradition. The commercial spin-offs are equally impressive, sprawling wedding grounds, allied creative businesses creating fashions, setting trends, and commanding reams of coverage in the popular media – all made possible by the more liberal economic climate of the 1990s, which changed Indians in a fundamental way. And yet, despite the outward change, the inherent traditions and wedding rituals, including where the bride and groom stand in the pecking order, haven't changed all that much.

The next question that needs to be addressed is whether marriage remains relevant to the new urban Indian? The question emerges from a shifting reality brought about by varying doses of globalization, social media, economic demands and new forms of love and intimacies – all of which are changing the urban Indian in fundamental ways, which we are still in the throes of processing. Even so the answer to the above question seems to be a resounding 'Yes!' A vast majority of the Indian society still believes that marriage is the most popular way of finding companionship, and securing other must-haves like children, financial security, etc. And while it remains an important marker of caste, identity, community and culture, the institution of marriage continually adapts itself to the desires of the millennials, who form a large chunk of our population.

Statistics too back this belief. According to the 2011 census conducted by the Government of India, 49.9 per cent of the total number of women in the country see marriage as a part of their adult destiny.[5] Giving teeth to this statistic is the fact that approximately 92 per cent women have tied the knot by the time they are 25, and it goes up to 96 per cent by the time they are 29. The men by contrast have more leeway, presumably with economics being more central to their adult destiny, with only 42 per cent of the total male population married between 20 and 28 years of age.[6](A large percentage of the population is not represented here because they were outside the age bracket profiled in the survey.)

What is it about our social and cultural background that makes marriage so central to our lives? We also need to understand how it evolved within the sociocultural space, its links to religion, the historicity of certain traditions and rituals, the interconnections with love and romance, and its changing identities and avatars as the system adapts to the impatient demands of a younger generation.

But while socially-sanctified unions occupy a huge amount of space in our collective mindscape, in literature and the media, the otherness of the unconventional – the alternate forms of love and togetherness, too need their share of the stage lights. Juxtaposed with the stories of marriage are also those of single people, whether once married or never, who have developed a marvellous insulation to the pressures exerted by a marriage-obsessed society and seek other forms of companionship.

These various strands come together to present a fascinating narrative of the love lives of the adult world and its relationship with the Indian wedding, which remains at its core, a leviathan, an ever-transformative institution that both shapes and in turn is moulded by a dynamic social structure and shifting economics.

To understand why weddings play such a dominant role in the Indian imagination we have to begin by looking at the Indian wedding in its historical context, the traditions and rituals behind it, even as we continue to examine how it is shaped by contemporary influences – the social media, soaring aspirations, a growing economy – in a country that has one of the youngest populations in the world, with 45 per cent of the population belonging to the 15-40 age group (census 2011)[7] or a whopping 585 million, which is nearly twice the overall population of the United States. This youth leads the sentiments of the wedding market, with hundreds of thousands of weddings taking place every year across the country. Barring a few 'inauspicious' days, weddings are a year-round affair, fanning an insatiable appetite for wedding-related goods and services, giving rise to new businesses, while propping up the traditional ones.

For a long time now, Indians have been celebrating their weddings with an extravagance of style and scale, dwarfing every other social event in their lives. Weddings these days are carefully managed under the steady gaze of the social media, where every blink of the eye and every smile lighting up the face of the bridal couple is extensively published on various apps, begging for 'likes' and comments – a never-seen-before phenomenon that has affected every socioeconomic class in this country. And yet this is only the tiny, visible tip of the vast social-media-using population in the country, as mobiles and the internet connectivity continue to span wider horizons.

To truly understand this crisscrossing of the old and the new, the traditional value systems with modern and alternate beliefs, we first need to delve into that monolith, that red-flag warning on every cultural map lest we subvert it, the overarching theme of a thousand political debates – 'Indian culture'. Since its complexity and vastness precludes the possibility of confining ourselves to one-line answers, we resort to the encyclopedic internet. Google immediately throws up some 2,14,00,00,000 results for 'Indian culture' in 0.76 seconds! Most searches mention the philosophy, festivals, religion and languages of India to define the term, accompanied with the commendation, 'Indian culture is unique and varied'. Another tells us that it has become 'renowned all over the world'.

Sociologists like Irawati Karve[8] point out that in order to understand any cultural phenomenon in India one must understand its two foremost components – the 'configuration of the linguistic regions and the institution of caste and the family organization' – all of which are intricately linked and together form the scaffolding of what constitutes Indian culture.[8] Without going into too much detail, we can get some understanding of this rationale from the following example. In some regions south of the Vindhyas, many castes give preference to marrying one's elder sister's daughter or the father's sister's daughter, according to Karve. And if that's not possible, then the option is to marry the maternal uncle's daughter. This practice of cross-cousin marriage spills over into many other communities as well, the rationale being that if a family has taken a daughter, then they must also return a daughter to the same family. In north India such a practice would be considered taboo, and most communities would balk at the idea of such an alliance. In large swathes of northern India, marital alliances are rooted in the system of *gotra*, which we will discuss later.

This book finds its rationale in the singular argument that the country's vast young population believes in marriage, and that they will get married at some point in their adult lives. It is important to examine where this impulse springs from. Promilla Kapur, a sociologist writing about contemporary India says, 'In the past two decades or so there have been profound changes in the attitudes of the people of India towards various aspects of life ... with almost sacrosanct social institutions ... and conscious attitudes towards love, marriage and sex.' These changes will be critically examined in this book.[9]

As we have seen, culture and philosophy, modern beliefs and ancient wisdom, form a fusion of arguments that endorse the tradition of marriage in India. According to the shastras[10] such as the Dharmasutras, the Arthshastra, the Kama Sutra and the Upanishads, marriage is an integral element to realize at least three of the four purusharthas or objects of human pursuits. These four life goals for human beings according to the Hindu way of life are: dharma or the right way of life, kama or the erotic element in life, artha or material wealth, and moksha or salvation.

To this day, certain marriage customs and norms are rooted in traditions that are mentioned in the scriptures. Some of these customs can even be traced back to the two major Sanskrit epics – the Ramayana by Rishi Valmiki and its later version, Tulsidas' Ramcharitmanas,[11] and the Mahabharata by Rishi Vyas. Marriage within the parameters of caste, the ties of kinship and certain customs go back to ancient times. The giving away of the daughter and her patrilocal absorption into her husband's family, as was the case for Sita (in the Ramayana) and Draupadi (in the Mahabharata), continues in the modern world. Eight various kinds of marriages were approved by Manu, who has given a detailed road map of the Hindu way of life in his book, the Manusmriti.[12] Marriage was governed by the rituals that were linked in turn to varna or caste. Manu defines these eight forms of marriage and how they are to be conducted. His views reflect the primacy of the male, enjoining the giving away of the daughter (after bedecking her in finery and jewellery) by the father to her future husband through a sexist ritual known by its equally sexist term, '*kanyadaan*'.[13] The detailed instructions on the division of varna is equally problematic as well, and needs to be scrutinized more closely. One of the forms of the wedding mentioned by Manu, is the *Gandharva* vivah, or marriage where the couple assert their own choice of partner. This form of marriage has won great plaudits in Vatsyayana's Kama Sutra[14] as the most beautiful way of uniting lovers. Shakuntala and Dushyant, whose love has been immortalized in Kalidasa's Abhigyan Shakuntalam,[15] had united in a *Gandharva* vivah. Such a marriage based on love between the two partners did not involve *kanyadaan*, but patriarchal interpretations have co-opted this ritual even in this form of the wedding in present times.

As India changes gears and steps up in the global economy, poised to become the fifth-largest economy in the world – displays of wealth are percolating into the tiniest niches of the sociocultural space, and forever altering our perceptions of life and lifestyles. With the world knocking on our doors and brandishing its glitziest goods, tempting our senses with the proverbial apple of untempered consumption, our subscription to Gandhian austerity, a legacy from post-Independence days, has been severely put to test. In the early 1990s when a crumbling economy required India to mortgage her gold reserves, the then Prime Minister Narasimha Rao and Finance Minister Manmohan Singh loosened the shackles of red-tapism and bureaucracy and brought in liberalization of the economy.[16] Soon enough, economic indicators became buoyant, translating into visible signs of a growing economy: the Sensex jumped, the one-airline dominated sky opened up, pot-holed roads turned into highways crawling with gleaming automobiles, not merely the soup can version of the Ambassador car, and banks offered softer loans with a smile.

Into this well-greased promise of wealth stepped the middle-classes, who had the education and the skills needed to transform their personal fortunes, while the downsides of unequal growth were masked under the ritzy gizmos and facades of 'the dil maange more' culture.

An unstoppable change was happening across India with ambition and acquisition becoming the twin mantra propelling the country's youth to the new IT hubs – Bengaluru, Hyderabad, Gurgaon, Chennai, Pune and others springing up in different corners of the country. Their mofussil origins posed few obstacles to their soaring dreams. They embraced the anonymity of big cities, adopting its fluidity, the unyoking from caste and community tags. Fortunate and free, they found the breathing spaces to meet, interact and fall in love with someone not sanctioned by the parental figure. To this potent world of possibilities was added the addictive thrust of the social media, smart-phones came next, and the world turned on its axis.

More than ever before, young women and men said no to deeply entrenched conventions of religion, caste and class. In north India, the dreaded *gotra* system, which disallows marriage between those from the same sub-castes, was given the thumbs-down at the peril of questioning a community's honour and even getting killed for it. In real terms, it meant that when a Brahmin politician's daughter Sakshi Mishra married a Dalit, one of the lowest castes in the pecking order, she was hounded by her father and his goons. She was so worried for the safety of her husband and her own life that she went on a defiant social media rampage, declaring that if anything were to happen to them then her father should be held responsible for it. She says, 'Live and let live. Stop harassing my husband and his family … I want to be free and I want to be happy.'[17]

This call for freedom and happiness echoes elsewhere too. For example, Akbar, from an eminent Muslim family from Lucknow, known to me, met Minakshi Jain in management school and the two fell in love. The wall threatening their relationship was their food preferences – he couldn't live without meat, and she gagged even if garlic and onion were served on the table. For the sake of love, the young man gladly gave up the delicacies of Lucknowi Nawabi cuisine and turned vegetarian, earning his wife's grateful love and smiles. But the decision sent shockwaves across the aristocratic Nawab's family and his mother confided in me, her beautiful patrician features clouded with disappointment, 'What will happen to our precious recipes handed down through the generations? So painstakingly learnt, so secretively guarded within the family kitchen – who will cook them, who will ever enjoy those delicacies?' The mother, in her despair, voiced a deep-rooted concern that shows the tension between traditions and the adaptation to a new social order. She could accept her son pushing the boundaries of their religious order by marrying a Hindu or a Jain, but when it threatened the continuity of familial traditions – the kernel that communities guard so zealously – her adaptability was pushed to the limit.

Such stories, increasingly a sub-plot in the grand unfolding of the Indian wedding scenario, are pointers to a tectonic social shift in a society, which has hitherto operated on firm codifications of caste. The accident of birth determined who stood where in the social hierarchy, who was marriageable and who was forbidden. Arundhati Roy articulates this tension in *The God of Small Things*, where she defines the love laws, 'the laws as that lay down who should be loved, and how. And how much.'

The prescriptive diktat for 'love' hasn't gone out of vogue either, despite the challenge that fugitive love periodically poses to it. And so we have the phenomenon of elopements, where a couple judged unsuitable on the touchstones of caste and community, run away and get married secretly.[18] The chapter 'Breaking Love Barriers' examines precisely that – the growing incidence of young love refusing to be thwarted either by elders or by the rigid templates of caste and class. But there's a price to be paid for such rebellion – hounded by kith and kin, battling the spectre of 'honour killing', couples go on the run seeking the alternative safety nets set up by the state and the courts, with a plexus of touts seeing them through the tumultuous passage of marrying for love. The chapter also looks at sexuality and erotica that is so entwined in religious texts, and expresses itself in various art forms as the *rasa* or essence of *shringar*.[19]

And yet a large percentage of the country's youth want traditional weddings, with the parental stamp of approval sealing his/her choice of partner.[20,21] A clear divide shows itself between classes – as my survey of some fifty young women and men across the metropolitan cities reveals, 90 per cent of respondents from upper-class families want to marry for love, while the youth from smaller towns still favour arranged marriage.

The chapter 'Arranging Love' looks at the choppy terrain of marriage arranged along the lines of community, class, caste, financial and educational strata, and the parents' role as they try to find the right partner for their adult progeny, 'a peculiar prerogative appropriated by South Asian parents'. This is where one most closely sees a peculiar tension that is stirring the hearts of young India, the backlash from the older generation, the tightening of caste and class rules, and the great conundrum of giving freedom to one's girls and yet expecting their unquestioned adjustment to outdated roles of submission. The collective genuflection at the altar of Mammon – everyone wants a great job and white goods collectibles like the latest TV and mobiles, and yet the mindset still reeks of mothballs. As Lata, a young woman working as a sales girl in a showroom in Bhopal, says after breaking off her engagement, 'The guy wanted me to be hi-fi and wear only jeans and western clothes, but his parents wanted a pallu on my head, and a dumb act where I wouldn't open my mouth before the in-laws.'

After the marriage is finally fixed, one way or another, we arrive at the extravaganza unleashed during the 'Big Fat Indian Wedding', a term gaining greater traction to describe the event as a flashy, grand celebration where wealth inflates traditional rituals into mega events, with the bridal couple sometimes lost in its glitz.[22] This is the subject of the next chapter: 'Weddings and the Kiss of Money'.

And from the big wedding to the seamless twist that the country's skewed power equation leads to – the dowry, in the chapter, 'The Devil is in the Dowry'. Dowry as opposed to *streedhan* – there's a huge chasm separating the two – is a forced extraction of money and goods demanded by the groom's family. While *streedhan* is personal wealth bequeathed to a woman, for her to spend as she desires, and that no one else can appropriate. The dowry menace is single-handedly responsible for devaluing women and by extension the girl child. This is reflected in the skewed gender ratio in India which is one of the worst globally. It burdens the woman's parents in unimaginable ways, with the quality of groom directly linked to the size of the dowry and the scale of the wedding that the parents can muster. The Hindi phrase employed by marriage brokers hits home with its raw crudity, 'The quantity of ghee is directly proportional to the ferocity of the fire.' In other words, parents are warned not to be stingy about the dowry, if they want their daughter to make a match of it.

But dowry is not merely about securing the best match. This evil practice, fanned by ravenous greed, consumes hundreds of young lives. Dowry-related deaths are so routine that very rarely does the news item move beyond the inner pages of newspapers, nor do they figure in the 'forwards' that social media thrives on, inured perhaps to its all-too-frequent occurrence in our ugly everyday. One wonders, why is the power equation so plainly tilted in favour of the groom's side?

While there are no easy answers, the demographic divide between women and men makes the situation even more baffling. Social norms and economics have an enormous bearing in fashioning such attitudes, added to which is the even more puzzling phenomenon that when it comes to finding a 'suitable boy,' the number of available men is tiny on the matrimonial chart.[23] Besides, everyone wants to corner that 'promising boy' as women are required to marry 'up', in order to establish their own social status. As one would ask at the end of a well-contested debate: what is the solution? There are no easy answers, yet the changing attitudes amongst the millennials may show the way forward.

What would a modern Indian wedding be without its generous share of Bollywood songs and dances, its ode to romantic love and its soaring, imaginative play of the arts? Bollywood today is that one element of Indian culture that is more identifiable across the world than most of our other exports. Not surprisingly therefore, when Indian weddings, enabled by deeper pockets, began changing into the grand spectacles of today, one of its smaller events, 'The Ladies Night' wriggled out of the clutches of its limited nomenclature, gave a big grand hug to Bollywood and jumped to near-centrestage of the wedding celebration. It grabbed its own billing in invitation cards, cornered a generous share of the budget, and took its bow as the Sangeet. Everyone is now more enthused about the evening of fun, as opposed to the tradition-encumbered finale – the wedding ceremony. The chapter 'Bollywood Masala' pays tribute to this entwined legacy of weddings and films, exploring and analyzing a few chosen films that have had a lasting influence on weddings, especially in north India.

The various threads related to marriage examined in this book do show the primacy of the traditional notions of family and marriage between a man and a woman, yet there are some deviations. To quote Dr Henrike Donner, 'There's such a diversity in how marriages work in India that one cannot say that there is one kind of Indian marriage. There is still the strong idea that marriages should be arranged, heterosexual, and lifelong unions.'[24]

No book on weddings and marriages can justify its theme, without exploring romantic love, even though Indian marriages are built mostly on the premise of arranged matches, as surveys have shown,[25] with tick marks accorded on the basis of shared social attributes. This is what arranging a marriage means. Love, the stuff of dreams and Bollywood fantasies, is expected to emerge from the creative chambers of the labour room, once the children arrive, or a subsidiary of the *saptapadi*, where partners exchange vows of duty and commitment.

These two words – duty and commitment – forming the crux of a marriage, sounds peculiar for a civilization that has historically worshipped at the altar of romantic love, gathering the skeins of religion, philosophy, poetry, music and dance to create a bouquet of *shringar*, the *rasa* of erotica and love. The divine love between Parvati and Shiva or the beauty of play between Radha and Krishna, has been described as the purest, most distilled form of love.

Religion and erotica make an explosive combination in temple art too, as witnessed in the sculptures of Khajuraho and Konark, both declared UNESCO World Heritage Sites. The exquisite sculptures and their depictions of the most imaginative erotica, with no taboos inhibiting the sculptor's chisel, are known all over the world. Kama or the erotic, is the theme of Vatsyayana's *Kama Sutra*, the earliest and most detailed treatise on the art of lovemaking, whose relevance on bookshelves remains unquestioned to this day. Witness the lovelorn Yaksha imploring the cloud as messenger to travel to his wife in *Meghdutam*. Kalidas's many poems are intense odes to love, as are Bhartrihari's love poems.[26]

Though a book about weddings, this work must look at the alternate worlds created by those who choose to stay out of the marriage circle. There are huge swathes of people who have never married out of choice or their orientation has not permitted them to do so, since same-sex marriages are yet to be recognized under Indian law,[27] or who remain single because of religious calling. There are also others who have opted out of the institution. Their space is equally significant and the chapter: 'The Singular Life: Marriage from the Other Side', is a look at these alternative voices.

The impulse to write this book, other than its seed in a childhood memory, has other origins too. It began with a need to go beyond the outer trappings of customs and rituals, the incomprehensible Sanskrit and a collage of images of the 'good life' – happy faces, beautiful clothes, the feasts, the music, some teary moments, and a couple becoming partners for life. But what connects the different customs and rituals, where lies their historical or scriptural origins, which interpretations have shaped them further, remains unclear. As also how marriages, and their customs, rituals and the gender perceptions are interwoven into the historical and the prevailing social and cultural realities.

The contemporary wedding is also a marvellous display of packaging, which pays its obeisance to market forces. As weddings have become grander and glitzier, the economics and the customs have become inseparable. But economics have only accentuated a fundamental inequality – the imbalance between the bride's and the groom's side, where the former has to pick up the tab for most of the expenses, including gifts for the groom's side. The coercive demand for dowry in some weddings, amplified by India's rising consumerism, is of course its ugliest expression. The unequal power equation is also woven into many of the rituals, their countless repetitions numbing us into accepting them unquestioningly as a part of the wedding covenant. While looking for an apt quotation from the scriptures as an inscription for this book, it was truly difficult to find one that did not impose a male-centric view, or where the bride was not a responsibility handed from one male to another. This only underlines the need to identify the sexist overtones, as a prelude to moving away from or neutralizing them – a debt owed to future generations.

This book though is designed along the lines of a vedic ritual – the *saptapadi* – imbued with the symbolic and the sacred, as the bridal couple goes around the *agni kund* to the recital of mantras. It's also instantly recognizable as a rite that is practiced across regions, and therefore seemed like the perfect template for this book.

Much of the data quoted in this book has been gleaned from primary and secondary sources. The former includes discussions, interviews and surveys amongst a cross-spectrum of people. I was particularly interested in understanding the perspective of the youth, who as protagonists are in many ways central to the wedding narrative. They are also the influencers of the future who will stamp their choices on how the wedding culture is shaped, how it is woven into social mores and in turn impacts the family. To this end I interviewed young people in Bengaluru, Delhi and Kolkata. I was also conscious of the need to account for lower socio-economic groups, who live on the margins of our cities and societies, and who mentally and emotionally straddle the mofussil towns they have left behind and the metropolitan cities where they currently reside. And so, with the help of our NGO, Women Work & Health Initiative, which runs a community educational centre in the Sangam Vihar area, one of the largest unauthorized areas in south Delhi, I collated the views of some 50 women in the age group of 18-30 years regarding their views on marriage. On some broad issues the responses were remarkably similar between the underprivileged and the rich, showing how each borrows from the other, though social attitudes are more circumscribed, less elastic, more driven by economic issues amongst the poor, including the age when girls marry, which still is very young. I also tried to get the views of other stakeholders involved in the wedding process – extended families, those who have firmly turned down marriage, LGBTQIA persons, wedding designers, lawyers, social scientists, teachers, beauticians and others. This book has also been informed by my own work and interactions as a social entrepreneur working closely with women and development, as a writer and editor of books on gender, and lastly but importantly, as a parent who is privy to seeing this world through a youthful lens.

This attempt to deconstruct the Indian wedding by looking at the intersectionality of the historical, cultural and social dynamics that have shaped it, and which sparks a ripple effect across an arc of fashion, food, music, movies etc. was definitely a challenging, but also a hugely rewarding journey. I hope it will be the prequel for greater engagement with some of the questions raised here, even as the celebrations continue.

1

TOEING THE LINE: MARRIAGE AS A LIFE-CHANGER

Everybody loves a good wedding. Taking a cue from Jane Austen, one can say it is a truth universally acknowledged, that in India people are either getting married, are waiting to get married, or if already married, they are planning and plotting the marriage of those poor souls who are yet outside its blanket embrace. Anybody between the age of 20-30 years, or as the great Indianism goes 'of marriageable age', can hardly escape the well-meaning, though often annoying, intentions of all and sundry to pair them off. The going gets tougher by the time one reaches the 'beyond marriageable age' (over 30) bracket. A decided breach of accepted social behaviour, being single provokes varied reactions on the lines of – 'Unpardonable!' 'Aaj kal ke bachche', 'Kids these days are unreasonable, too individualistic' – all attributed to Western influences. It's a supposed vacuum which gives perfect strangers and related aunties and uncles the latitude to ask, 'But beta, when?' or darkly imply 'Is something wrong?' Single people even from other cultures find themselves subjected to this concern. A young European woman, who was posted as a diplomat in India, shared stories of how her Indian friends were constantly trying to set her up, even going to the extent of orchestrating 'chance' meetings – the staple of the arranged marriage, where festivals and pujas, other people's weddings and family functions are employed to engineer that 'chance' meeting. It would seem that there is simply no escape from this vigilantism.

Marriage: A Prescription of Sorts

Ancient Hindu texts prescribe four major stages in everyone's life. It is the second stage – *Grihasth ashram* – fulfilling one's dharma as a householder and having children, that lends marriage its relevance.[1] Marriage is an essential life event in the Indian psyche. With changing perceptions, many have rejected the institution, but they are considered aberrations, not the norm. Even as the winds of globalization waft into the country, changing the work culture, creating new demands, and ushering in seismic shifts in the way Indians eat, work, shop and travel, some elements have remained largely unchanged. One of them is the view that a person is 'unsettled' unless he or she is married. Single people, whatever their age, aren't considered to be independent units. Even a wedding invite to a single person is usually clubbed along with the rest of the family. In other words, it means that she or he does not merit an individual invite, unless they have established their own happy twosome with children in the works.

Marriage is seen almost as an achievement, with women especially being recognized by their marital status, rather than their academic or professional achievements. Sometimes it is proclaimed as a prescriptive medicine with wondrous curative powers. In some conservative families, if one has a son with a roving eye or lacks interest in his career, a bevy of elders are likely to advise, 'Get him married and he will be okay.' For girls, it's touted as even more of a panacea. Moody, depressed, disinterested in studies, and not doing anything concrete at home? 'Get her married and she will be all right!'

Parents traditionally view marrying off their children as their ultimate responsibility, irrespective of how well their children are doing professionally or how content they are with their personal lives. If unmarried, they are viewed as not being 'settled' yet. The opposite and worrying state of being 'unsettled' isn't just a concern about their child being partner-less, but also about 'What will people say?' From the time the child is born, entire families start anticipating the time when the baby-turned-adult would be wedded. The excitement is greater if the child in question has a special position in the family hierarchy – the eldest of the generation, or the first daughter, or an only son.

It would seem that in India most young people do wish to get married, or at least see it as an unquestionable part of one's adult life. Public segregation of the sexes is still practiced in large pockets of the society, making it hard for young people to meet, interact and have an intimate relationship outside of marriage. While these social norms are becoming less restrictive with time, marriage continues to be the best possible option to have close interactions with a significant other. Popular culture adds to the perception of the wedding as the event that truly announces a man or a woman's transition into adulthood.

Those few who defy this obsessive compulsion and say no to marriage, are subjected to all manners of peer pressures, pleas and even emotional blackmailing. When all other inducements fail, then the Gods are enlisted for good measure, by way of yagnas, havans and fasts. The *mannat* or vow is another favourite strategy adopted by the seekers to appease the gods and make that much-awaited wedding happen. Indians don't view individualism as a virtue, and have even less patience for those who profess quirky and unconventional behaviour. Therefore, most single people are badgered with a battery of reasons to get married. The number one reason continues to be 'getting settled'. This is followed closely with the idea of having your own family (read children), and thus securing the family line. While these reasons are used for both sexes, their details are different for men and women. In the case of the latter, there is the often-articulated need to transfer one's daughter's responsibility to another man and securing her financially, following Manu's greatly skewed edict that a woman is always dependent on a man. And so, a woman must marry and find her 'real home' with her husband. This dated notion is unfortunately dinned into the ears of little girls all the way into adulthood, conditioning them to a future that must include marriage. For boys, while they feel proprietorial in their parents' homes, there is constant pressure to build a safe and financially-rewarding career so they can provide for their imaginary families.

In a group conversation with domestic workers living in a poor unauthorized colony in Delhi, aged between 18-40 years, most of whom had little education and were married early, marriage remained an inextricable part of their destiny, an unquestionable decision made by the elders. But there was a definite attitudinal shift in the responses of the older women who saw marriage as burdened by responsibility, as opposed to the younger lot, who were enthusiastic about the idea of love and having a man to call their own. But across the board the future looks different. Most of the women declared that they would like their daughters to complete their education and marry only after that, 'but not too late, otherwise we will not get a good boy'. There were a few single women too in their late-thirties. A couple of them had never married because their parents were too poor to provide a dowry and their earnings helped support their families. They expressed hardly any regrets about being single, preferring their freedom and the independence provided by their income, without being at the beck and call of a man, they added.

For men too, marriage remains big on their radar. Families expect them to get married by a certain age, though it's shorn of the compulsive urgency or anxiety accorded to women. There is a reversal of expectations too. While a daughter's marriage has to be buttressed with money and goodies, the son's is the celebratory buntings adding to the family wealth.

Unfortunately, there is still a lot of stigma attached to people with alternative sexual preferences. Those who are unable to come out of the closet, or combat the immense pressure to get married, sometimes end up getting married to a heterosexual partner, in a bid to camouflage their preferences. Of late, the media has reported many such stories, of endless frustration triggered by such arrangements.[2] As one article reporting on the tragic consequences of these marriages puts it: 'In these cases, both man and woman were victims of a culture where people are expected to be married, bear children, acquire property, and contribute to the growth of the family lineage.'[3]

Then there are a few of those who opt out of the mainstream to pursue the calling of the soul, embracing religion and celibacy, instead of the *grihasth* life. The much-married adore them, flock to their *pravachans* or religious talks to resolve their worldly woes, and generously add to their 'donation boxes', but the ascetic's life is not for them.

The Beginnings

Marriage is deeply embedded in human social dynamics, with every religion, sect and community endorsing it. But what needs to be asked is how did this system evolve? Where did it begin, who set the rules? Anthropologists theorize that the concept of marriage evolved almost organically, with cross-cultural influences, until it reached the present state. Social scientists add that the family unit existed long before women and men really had a grasp of the term 'marriage' or how it was supposed to organize their social order. One is curious about the ancient civilizations – were people polygamous or monogamous, matriarchal or patriarchal, was adultery an alien concept, or was one free to choose to have sex with whomever one fancied? There are several theories about how life was lived in these undocumented times, how marriage evolved and functioned in its nascency. For example, Friedrich Engels, a nineteenth-century social critic of capitalistic economies and patriarchal families, argued that matriarchal families existed in early primitive societies.[4] It was the community that owned property, sexual relations were casual, and the family, when it was distinct from the larger group, was defined as mothers and their children.[5] Other nineteenth-century theorists were convinced that primitive man had established a system of group marriage, where men and women had a free choice of partners, society was egalitarian, with the children born from these unions taken care of by the community.[6,7] Social scientists are more cautious in their assessment of early societies and marriage, and write that 'from the societal point of view, marriage is an institution that serves to ensure propagation and socialization of children of a particular society'. The first recorded evidence of marriage ceremonies uniting one woman and one man dates from about 2350 B.C., in Mesopotamia. Over time marriage evolved into a widespread institution embraced by the ancient Hebrews, Greeks, and Romans. Its primary aim was to bind women to men, and establish that the children were truly his biological heirs. The early tribals and Anglo-Saxons saw marriage as a strategic tool to establish diplomatic and trade ties, says Stephanie Coontz, author of *Marriage, A History: How Love Conquered Marriage*. By the eighth century, with the Catholic Church becoming more powerful, marriage was viewed as a sacrament that earned God's grace. The idea of romantic love was born perhaps in the Middle Ages, its model based on the tale of the knight who felt an intense love for someone else's wife, as in the case of Sir Lancelot and King Arthur's wife, Queen Guinevere.

Coming to the Indian context, ancient texts such as the Vedas and the Puranas,[8] have several stories about how men and women lived together before the conjugal relationship was formalized. Interestingly, some of these are in line with Engels' theory. Early texts such as the Anushasana Parva in the Mahabharata, describe a time when relations between men and women were more flexible and there was no prohibition on who could sleep with whom.[9] There were no taboos on sex even amongst close relatives, the rationale being that one should have the most fertile partner in order to have many children, who were seen as a source of wealth and added to the status of the family. But as the population grew and the need for such freely-sanctioned sex became less urgent, relationships became more structured. And yet the dos and don'ts were not particularly rigid, as the following verse from the Rig Veda illustrates.[10] Here we have Yami telling her twin brother Yama, of her sexual need for him, but when he refuses, she berates him roundly with the following words:

'किं भ्राता सद्यद् अनाथं भवति? किम् स्वसा यत् निरऋतिः न गच्छात्'

What is (the use of) brother, who keeps me Anaath (Uncovered/Unprotected)?
What is (meaning of being) Svasaa who cannot even follow her drive?

In the Mahabharata's Shanti Parva, we gain some very interesting insights into ancient life. Bhishma pitamah, the grand old patriarch, defeated by his own protégée Arjuna, lies awaiting his death at an hour of his own choosing, his body impaled on a bed of arrows. Sharing his ancient wisdom with Yudhishthira, the eldest Pandava, he tells him about the changing prism of the woman-man relationship through four different ages or yugas.[11]

न चैषां मैथुनो धर्मो बभूव भरतर्षभ
संकल्पादेवैतेषां अपत्यं उपपद्यते

ततः त्रेतायुगेकाले संस्पर्शात् जायते प्रजान
ह्य भूः मैथुनो धर्मस्तेषां अपि जनाधिप

द्वापरे मैथुनो धर्म प्रजानां भवन्नृपःतथा
कलियुगे राजन द्वन्द्व मापेदिरे जनाः

In Satya yuga, intercourse happened as desire arose in minds of fertile men and women. There were no words for mother, father, sibling etc. In Treta yuga, when men and women touched each other and welcomed the touch, dharma allowed them to copulate for the time being. (This is the stage where concept of 'favourite' mate started emerging). In Dwapara yuga, men and women started cohabiting as couples but not as stable and committed pair-bonding couples. In Kali yuga, the stable pair-bonding (what we refer to as institution of marriage) emerged.

The transition from Satya yuga to the present-day structure of the woman-man relationship, in many ways traces the increasing complexity of the socio-cultural world. From the primitive world of survival by the hunter-gatherer man, as the society became more structured, matriarchal identities began to take precedence with the offspring, free from patriarchal belongingness, coming to be known instead by their mother's name. And so lineages became linked to the mothers – such as the Aadityas (lineage of aditi), Daityas (lineage of Diti), Vainateyas (lineage of Vinita), Kaartikeyas (lineage of Kritikaa), Daanavas (lineage of Danu) and so on. Though these were all 'women of Prajapati' or the Lord of the Universe, the offspring did not take Prajapati's name.

Another example, which might be considered prurient even in today's world, has Bhishma telling Yudhishthira the story of Sudarshan Rishi, where even the holy sage is pleased to learn that his wife Oghavati, has fulfilled the dharma of the *grihastha* (the householder) and honoured their guest by having sex with him.[12] Over time, relationships underwent changes and as couples stuck together, women were more jealously guarded by their men. He cites the case of Ahilya in the Ramayana, where Rishi Gautama curses her for a supposed transgression and transforms her into a rock. She is later rescued only when Rama comes to her aid.

Bhisma's anecdotes show the gradual assertion of patriarchal mores, with the relationship between sexes getting stringently codified. Gautama and Ahilya are one example from the Ramayana. But Sita's chastity test, the *agni pariksha* or trial by fire, by her husband King Rama, has become a metaphor for women subjected to patriarchal judgements of 'purity'. A definite pattern is visible from these examples, with patriarchy defining social structures and allotting very specific roles for women. The target is women's sexual autonomy, which is squashed into a box with a man's name stamped on it, and so she becomes his property.

Throughout this long journey, where the woman-man relationship has been transformed from easy sexuality to this steady, rule-bound format, Hindu scriptures have unstintingly accorded Kama or the pursuit of pleasure, sex and erotica, as a primary pursuit of human existence, labelling it as one of the purusharthas, or the four goals of life, through which human beings can realize their full potential. There is another story in the Mahabharata where Yudhishthira, the wise one, asks his brothers which Purushartha demanded their greatest attention. Arjuna the master archer says artha, or material wealth, Yudhishthira unsurprisingly opts for dharma, the righteous way of life, while Bhim the pragmatist, argues that it is kama or sexual pleasure that he considered to be the most important, as there would be no human race to pursue these lofty ideals in its absence.

The Scholarly View

Understanding how marriage plays out in reality, particularly in the Indian scenario, is a long and complex endeavour. It has tested the wits of intellectuals and philosophers, who have given us a few guidelines to aid our understanding of the matter. Sarvepalli Radhakrishnan, philosopher and the second president of India, held a feminist view of marriage, which he says is overwhelmingly loaded against women. He said, 'Primitive marriage was based on the subjugation of woman, its durability rested on economic necessity not evanescent passion …' He viewed marriage as a social institution, not merely to give birth and nurture progeny, but whose 'main aim is the enrichment of the personality of husband and wife, through the fulfilment of their needs for a permanent comradeship.'[13] Swami Vivekananda's view is more practical, shorn of all the romantic ideals. He says, 'Marriage is not for a sense of enjoyment but to perpetuate the race.'[14]

The contemporary world has pushed marriage into a greater loop of expectations as illustrated by this example from Promilla Kapur in her book *Love, Marriage and Sex*, where a young woman when asked about her expectations of marriage replies, 'I wanted to marry … to have the satisfaction of material, physical and emotional needs, and to possess a husband, home, and children. I expected material comforts, physical satisfaction, love, companionship, sharing of interests ...'[15] In a group discussion with young women and men living in Kolkata I posed nearly an identical question regarding their expectations of marriage, if they planned to marry in the first place. Aged between 23–26 years, they were all in their first jobs, earning between ₹25,000 to ₹40,000 per month. Every one of them said that they would get married at some point in the future. Clearly, they were more focussed on shaping their careers before getting married. Some of them didn't give marriage too much importance, and instead considered it an individual's choice. But their expectations? The list ran along lines similar to that of Kapur's respondent decades ago. Girls saw in marriage the possibility of children and family, financial stability, a sex partner, a good life, as they saw this happening with some of their relatives. There was also the sense that it might affect their careers, with in-laws and husbands opposing their professional work. For men, happiness and responsibility seemed to be the two images of marriage that dominated their minds.

Though touted as the greatest adult institution by almost all major religions, marriage has come under fire as the ultimate bastion of patriarchy. Researchers and feminists find that traditional marriages are so biased towards men that women's lives, instead of becoming happier or easier after marriage, become burdened with household chores and the care work, which fall disproportionately in her lot.[16,17,18,19] The unfair division of household work means that the outside spaces, which are linked to money and power, belong to the man. For women, it is the home with all its nurturing duties that becomes her world. Care work as it is called, of children, the sick, the elderly, the household, finds no mention under the economically-driven activities that governments so painstakingly collect data about. It seems as if women do no work at all. Some researchers have indicated that this unequal distribution of wealth and power between men and women could lead to domestic violence, which may be exacerbated by marital concepts of entitlement and ownership. Mahatma Gandhi, the great visionary, could see the imbalance between female and male roles within the family structure. He saw it as the foundation that perpetuated the subordination of women and wrote caustically, 'Marriage is probably the oldest social institution and the most abused … In this unequal struggle of women against social tyrannies imposed on them, nothing has played so crucial a part as marriage. It is in fact the base from which the continuous attacks on them are made. For men it is a cloak which covers a multitude of their failings, the betrayals of their social obligations.'

Focussing on how this plays out in the desi scenario, we have Manu the misogynist, saying that it was perfectly permissible for the woman to be subordinated by the man. In the sphere of religion and spiritual growth, he gives men the desire and the direction, while for a woman the worship of her husband, was enough to transport her to the gates of heaven.

This version of the *pati* as *parmeshwar* (husband as God) has been cited so often in various commentaries of religious texts, that women too have internalized the idea, creating in due course a deep divide between the *sumangla*, or the woman with a husband, and its binary the *amangala*, the widow, sans one. The paranoia, that centuries of rabid discrimination against widows foments, isn't just because of the colourless state of the widows of Vrindavan, chanting endless paeans to Lord Krishna as their saviour, but other stark images add to it. The denuding of colour and jewellery from a woman's life in the wake of widowhood, have deep psychological ramifications. In order to stave off widowhood, women across the country observe various kinds of fasts like *Karwa Chauth*, *Hartalika Teej*, *Karadaiyan Nonbu*, *Gowri Vratam*, Monday and Thursday fasts etc. to keep their husbands breathing longer.[20] Certain ornamentations too are imbued with the marks of the marriage, like sindoor, glass bangles, mangalsutra, *taali*, *dejhoor* in Kashmir etc.

The imbalance of power equations is reinforced during the wedding ceremony, where many communities across Bengal, Bihar, Assam, Orissa and others have the bride touch her husband's feet. However, things are changing. At a recent wedding that I attended, the bride (in her thirties), who worked in a senior position in a well-renowned company, and the groom were finally taking the pheras, much to everyone's relief. On the completion of the seventh phera, which marked the end of the ceremony, the priest declared in stentorian tones, that the bride may now touch the groom's feet, much in the manner of a kiss sealing the relationship in a Christian ceremony. The bride's response was an unexpected and emphatic refusal, which threw the priest into a tizzy. He began moralizing on the merits of the act, while an equally flustered mother tried to convince her daughter. To end the matter, the groom, a handsome nerd, much amused by the furore, offered to touch the bride's feet instead. In the southern states, higher literacy has made people aware of some overtly sexist terminology, e.g. the *kanyadaanam* – a term which continues to be in vogue in north Indian weddings, was discarded in favour of the more descriptive *panigraham*, where the father gives away the bride.

Wedding – A Family Act

What else has changed in the wedding scenario? The scale and the drama. But the heart and soul of most Indian weddings has always been the getting together of close and distant family and friends. The celebration of weddings as an unbridled outpouring of money that draws wondrous gasps from the audience used to be a rare phenomenon, with only the truly wealthy industrial families or the landed gentry having the means to imagine such a preposterously expensive party. Most weddings, in the grand sweep of middle-class India, were solemnized within the parameters of the 'decent' wedding, as advertisers declared in matrimonial columns. Though marvellously vague and left strictly to the realm of interpretation, the phrase largely hints at a modest wedding. In those pre-liberalization decades – the 1970s, the 1980s and even the early 1990s – when India was a closed economy, weddings were mostly low-key and simple affairs. In many cases the invitees were expected to share their rooms with other guests, with hard mattresses laid out in neat rows on the floor as additional beds. Today's individual rooms in fancy hotels were unimaginable. Toilets were the ill-lit beacons at the end of long corridors, and food was a concoction conjured by the local cook, with the family's women, sari pallus tucked into their waists, would run back and forth from the kitchen overseeing the meals. Weddings in north India happening in the thick of the summer months had everyone perspiring, though the nostalgic types remember with great fondness the damp-straw smell of khus mats, that were supposed to provide some relief. In Tamil weddings too, women resplendent in the thick silk of Kanjeevaram saris, learnt to battle the heat for the sake of the sartorial, until later when marriage halls began sporting a few air-conditioners to everyone's relief. Drinking water used to be stored in large mud pots, while the cooling drinks like lassi and sherbet in the north and buttermilk in the south were generously infused with local and very questionable ice. All of these trimmings were secondary to getting together and guffawing with the extended family for a few days.

The changing times are introducing new ways of interpreting and practicing the institution of marriage, and though the joint family is no longer the monolithic arrangement it once was, with a dozen or so related members living under the same roof, the family remains central to any wedding. If the old adage 'You marry not just the person but the family' remains a truism in India even today, it is because there is a place accorded to every close family member in the enactment of the numerous wedding rituals. It's not limited to the father's role of the giving away the bride, the parents from either side have many ceremonies to perform – from the preparatory ones like anointing the bride/groom with oil, the haldi etc. to some key rituals in the main wedding ceremony. The extended family members too have specific roles in this grand happening. Brothers, sisters, uncles, aunts, brothers and sisters-in-law, are all accorded vital ceremonious roles in the enacting of the many rituals that lead to the actual wedding ceremony, followed by the sequels that add to the wedding. These small though momentous roles, whilst establishing the hierarchical positions of family members in the kinship ladder, also play a huge role in gluing relationships. At a subtler level, these roles help the new entrant into the family to form relationships and bonds with various members of their partner's family.

Liberalization and Young India – The Twain Meet

The Indian wedding in its new avatar, suitably embellished with the frills of money and packaged as a status symbol, has been forged on the anvil of India's economic explosion started in the 1990s. Weddings have become grander, the feasts are more elaborate and economics rules. This is true across the country. As the middle-classes saw more money flowing into their bank accounts than ever before, conspicuous consumption became the norm. Gandhian austerity of the post-Independence India was junked, and the need to buy and possess more became the new mantras.

In the brief span of about twenty-five years, India witnessed an extraordinary change in its landscape – land prices zoomed to stratospheric heights and the construction industry became a rampant juggernaut, hand in glove with the political coterie. Skylines in most cities changed, fancy gadgets entered the earlier spartan homes and foreign brands bulldozed their way into closed markets. The telecom sector boomed (though mired in political scandals), while a raft of MNCs and big businesses entered a virgin territory burgeoning with economic promise. Though this growth had several downsides, with peak unemployment and inequitable distribution of wealth only getting worse, middle-class India was looking decidedly prosperous. India's demographic dividend – its youth – was changing the face of the country. A young population with access to a disposable income loves the exciting, empowering feeling of spending money. And this newly consumerist middle-class India was ready to pour its wealth into its most dearly loved celebration – the wedding.

The wedding, in the Indian imagination, is the mother of all signifiers. The ultimate celebration of family, kinship and the coming together of a young couple, the wedding industry began to grow, and at last count it was a ₹33,000 crore business – a leviathan creature springing multiple arms reaching into every facet of the service industry, including wedding planning, hotels, catering, travel, gifting, photography and others that have never before been factored into a wedding – the entertainment and media business.[21] And these are just the supporting cast, the main headliners being the jewellery, clothes and the trousseau. High emotions and disposable incomes have joined forces to produce unforgettable expressions of the experience of a lifetime. Etched in memory, frozen in videos and photo albums, hashtagged on social media. The wedding party, and not just the marriage, has become the ultimate life-changer!

2

ARRANGING LOVE

She walked into the room, balancing a tray of glasses filled to the brim, ice cubes lending a musical clink to her demure gait. Six pairs of eyes followed her every move, mentally according tick marks, confirming the different attributes listed in the matrimonial ad with the person now dispensing the glasses. '20 years, beautiful fair, slim, tall, homely, well-versed in household management etc.' The 'seeing' session was in progress. He, the potential bridegroom, an engineer by profession, sat on the sofa, flanked by his smug parents, as they mulled whether to say yes or walkout. This scene – so typical of the 'boy sees girl' routine that precedes an arranged marriage – has been spoofed and parodied endlessly in popular sitcoms and Bollywood. Today, a more likely scenario would be to have a concerned parent sitting on the computer, intently scanning the matches thrown up by the matrimonial website, trying to figure out the best partner for their child. Sometimes the children are unaware of this endeavour, some reluctantly agree just to get their parents off their backs, and some truly believe that their parents know best. This scouting around for the suitable one, fills the parents with an exaggerated sense of responsibility and power as they script the future lives of their adult sons and daughters. There is endless vetting of potentials – some get rejected outright and some qualify for the next round. But can this process really ensure their children's happiness? Are they really capable of finding 'the one' perfect partner for their daughter or son? These loaded questions drive some parents to places where their equilibrium and equanimity are seriously tested. Even in the Ramayana, when no man was qualified enough to be a suitable groom for Sita, her father Raja Janaka purportedly asked similar questions with a familiar sounding puzzlement. Until of course, Rama strung Shiva's bow and was granted the honour of marrying Sita.

The parent, vested with the responsibility of finding the right partner, starts with a list of cultural and social qualifiers, such as caste, community, stature, family background, work profile, income, looks, complexion, height, etc. This mythical partner, blessed with all the right attributes, isn't easily found. Yet, it's a dream that most parents pursue in the initial stages, until reality bites and they gradually begin to discard one required attribute after the other, and some finally leave it to kismet to take over. But kismet notwithstanding, the match-making process begins with the premise that one is sure to find the ideal match for their child, the Rama-Sita combination – despite its controversial end.

Yet, one may ask why the guardians of educated adult progeny need to take on the responsibility of finding them a suitable boy or girl? Considering that the young adults today, are as smart and sassy as they come, aware of the education options best suited for their career path, and with envious determination to pursue their goals. This smart young brigade has definite ideas of what they want to do, along with an admirable mix of pragmatism, logic and a street-smart chutzpah. Not for them the drudgery of a lifetime of pushing files or bending over smoking stoves to feed a large family. The idea of others before self is passé. Yet, when it comes to making this most fundamental of life choices, the fulcrum of one's future, an unfathomably large number follow the tradition of relying on their parents to make the right choice for them.

A leading hotel chain conducted a survey called the Taj Wedding Barometer, of over 1,000 people in the age group of 18–35 years across ten cities in the country. The idea was to assess marriage trends and how the youth responded to the idea of getting married. The findings showed that despite the social media boom and pop culture projections of love and romance as a glamourized accessory essential to one's lifestyle, 75 per cent of Indians still prefer to have an arranged marriage. North India, with a more conservative social structure, has this figure jumping to 82 per cent! Of the women interviewed, 82 per cent stated a clear preference for parental choice in selecting a life partner.[1] Which isn't quite so surprising, considering that daughters are brought up with far more constraints than sons, their dependency stoked from childhood.

What influences our youth to set aside their enterprising, free-wheeling spirit to follow the well-trodden path of arranged marriages? Part of the answer lies in the deep socialization process, which is woven into the fabric of the close-knit extended Indian family, and its rootedness in the larger network of society. Marriages in India don't just bring two individuals together but are focused on bringing families closer as well, an arrangement that everybody endorses. The young too seem to believe in the cultural definition of marriage as a family affair, rather than an individual undertaking. Harmony and shared values arising from common backgrounds are seen as more important than individual attraction. Sociologists Sudhir Kakar and Katharina

Kakar explain this phenomena: 'Given the deep stratification of Indian society along the lines of caste, creed, hierarchy, social class and education, the young feel relieved that their parents would arrange their marriage and make the best selection within the available pool of eligible men and women within their caste, community and economic status.'[2] The common grounds provided by an arranged match – familiar customs, foods, relatives, incomes, etc. – also helps in negotiating the dark thicket of matchmaking. The upside is also that this aids the adjustment process with the new partner and family, a stand-in for what is seen as the variable element of love.

The Parent as Authority Figure

Such malleable moulding of the young, certainly doesn't happen in a vacuous space without an entire socio-cultural milieu subscribing to it. The seeds are sowed in childhood, when children are taught to obey an invisible family rulebook, with parents actively discouraging the seemingly undesirable traits of independence and assertion of one's views. When it comes to daughters, the disciplining fetters become even tighter, since a tarnished reputation would scupper her chances in the marriage market. 'Where are you going? Why? With whom?' are questions from interrogations that adolescent girls are subjected to routinely, as anxious parents try to protect her from the imaginary roadside Romeos, to the real threats of a rising crime graph against women. While some might deem this as anachronistic and echoing a musty mindset, it continues to be the unfortunate reality of a young woman's world. The prime minister of the country, Narendra Modi, poised on the ramparts of the Red Fort, delivering his first Independence Day address to the nation in 2014 asked, 'Parents ask a number of questions when a daughter goes out, but do they ever have the courage to ask their son about his friends or where is he going or why? After all a rapist is also someone's son.'[3] He highlighted the suffocating parental control over girls that typifies the discrimination in the upbringing between daughters and sons.

Parental authority is an accepted feature of children's lives all over the world. But in India it continues well into adulthood. It translates into interference in career decisions, choice of friends, dietary preferences, etc. Despite this over-involvement, the so-called transgressions like drinking, smoking and premarital sex must be surgically hidden from their view. Despite the changes happening in urban centres, large parts of India still have families that view even harmless interaction with the opposite sex with suspicion and deep unease. They jump to conclusions, imagine the 'worst', i.e. physical intimacy, and so, never ease their tight leashes.

Across India's big and small towns, the sight of young couples spending time together in public spaces is seen as an act of questionable morals. The media often carries stories of the lopsided public outrage caused by this provocation to public morality. Sometimes even the police are called in to correct the moral breach. Stories of young couples hounded out of parks or gory pictures of the punishment meted to those displaying love across communities have been shared in various media.[4,5] Sometimes this public gatekeeping of an individual's love life can quickly descend into a dystopian nightmare, where falling in love – unless it fits into the mould of the coded love laws – is asking for trouble. And sure enough, it arrives in an imaginatively sadistic range of actions from public humiliations to death threats.

The award-winning film *Masaan*, portrays a similar scenario with a chilling sense of reality.[6] The converging points of middle-class morality in a closed society, the young wanting to break free from its suffocating stranglehold and the exploitation by those invested with authority – it packs a punch because it is reminiscent of numerous such tales that happen all too frequently in the country. Though the law pronounces no moral judgement on young couples living together or having consensual sex, the moral brigade and public opinion conjure a hypocritical furore over the flouting of the imagined norms of our culture, our sanskriti.

An environment which fosters such a pervasive suspicion of the mingling of boys and girls, can hardly have its young find their own partners. They therefore need their parents to step in, while parents view the prospect as their ordained duty. Social scientists have pointed out that, 'arranging marriages of their adult progeny is a peculiarly south Asian intergenerational contract entered into by parents, leading to a mutual obligation between the generations.'[7] Equally, this obligation gives parents the opportunity to exercise power and control over their children, and also gives them the possibility of pushing the interests of the family further. This keeps parental involvement in arranging matches a tightly-protected privilege in India.

In recent times, the arranged marriage system has received some flak from different quarters. 'It is a patriarchal artifact invested in maintaining caste purity, class privileges and gender hierarchy,' say several feminist scholars,[8] and some even talk about the tyranny of the household on women.[9] They recognize both – the global phenomena where the 'institution of family (is) one of the strongholds of female oppression', and the desire to create a new kind of family, one that 'would provide the individual's choices in coming together and building a relationship on their own terms, and not on terms handed to them by antiquity, traditions, ideology – most of which stemmed from patriarchy or male attitudes to female capabilities and roles.' The traditional, conservative family certainly fails to live up to any of the ideals that would foster gender equality, and is a far cry from the structure that feminist scholars visualize.

Matchmaking In Progress

In keeping with the times, marriages are being arranged like sophisticated ventures, designed to cater to the whims of their exclusive clientele. But since the demand cuts across classes, the old practices of arranging matches have not been altogether scrapped. The broker who brings potential alliances to the family, is as much a part of the matchmaking process as the newer approaches. In the uncertain days before marriage portals and dating websites, the broker, whether the family pandit or a professional matchmaker, was the go-to person who knew all about eligible bachelors and marriageable girls in the catchment society. Today's more competitive environment has only stretched their capabilities further. From bribing officers to gain access to the lists of young men qualifying for government jobs to whiling away hours outside an educational institution in order to convince a young man, about the desirability of a particular match – nothing stops the broker's ingenuity in her bid to deliver.

And what would the arranged marriage scenario be without relatives? Given India's complex network of families, relatives are often best placed to find an eligible match for a niece or a cousin's grandchild. Often, they know the prospective family personally or are connected to someone who is intimately so linked. This reassures the parents that they are not treading in completely unknown territory. They are also encouraged by the thought that their son or daughter would have a partner who has similar sanskaar, good genes, learned behaviour, generosity and grace handed down by the family.

Advertising for a Bride or a Groom

Matrimonial columns in the newspapers are another hallowed tradition in the quest to find a life partner, with some tracing it back to the era when the first newspapers started getting published in the country. In those early days, it was perhaps a gigantic technological leap from the limited reach of the broker or the relative. A common script runs through them, almost as if it is a programmed response to what the Indian mind constitutes as ideal. Only fair, slim, homely girls please. Matching of castes (jati or community as opposed to varna) continues to be a big requirement specifically mentioned in these ads, as Nobel Prize winners Abhijit Banerjee and Esther Duflo recorded in a study.[10] After analyzing the dataset from interviews with 783 matrimonial ads placed in a prominent Bengali newspaper, they arrived at the following conclusion: 'while caste is highly valued in terms of preferences, it does not require a very high price in equilibrium. These conditions appeared to hold in the data that we collected for arranged marriages in West Bengal. However, there are trends that suggest that caste-based preferences might be changing … Despite the value placed on caste and its low equilibrium price, 30 percent of people in our sample do not marry within their caste.'

These days, the men too have to be fair and handsome, prompting the Shahrukh Khans and John Abrahams of the movie industry to step onto the advertising bandwagon for male fairness creams.[11] But that is only an add-on. A man's attractiveness remains firmly anchored in his current and prospective income, and his family's wealth. Doctors, lawyers, engineers, management professionals are safe bets for whom the bride's parents are often willing to shell out a suitable dowry. And though other sectors have flourished in the last two decades, there are few takers for them in the traditional marriage market. What are the men looking for remains a question that occupies huge spaces in the matchmaking maze. Besides the paramount good looks, education too features high on the list. Whether the girl wants to work professionally or not is still a question that some families ask, though teaching or a government job evokes less angst. However, there is a burgeoning section of prospective grooms, who prefer having a working wife to share the burden of today's demanding economic realities.

India's social structures, riddled with contradictions, continue to harbour a utopian idea of the ideal girl. She is someone who is attentive and dutiful at home, a perfect wife and daughter-in-law, but in the outside world she should metamorphose into a smart, modern woman, a gracious hostess and perfectly at ease in social gatherings.

Matchmakers in Cupid's Role

Despite their popularity, matrimonial ads only complement other routes of matchmaking, one of which is the marriage bureau. Despite stiff competition from online portals, these bureaus are mushrooming across cities, fulfilling a pervasive need plaguing their rich, insecure clientele. Having made inroads into the turf of traditional brokers, whose provincial trappings didn't quite appeal to upper-class jetsetters, the marriage bureau conduits have had an image makeover. Their business dealings are as quick and savvy as their dress code – bespoke suits and Montblanc pens clipped to their pocket – they mean business, as proven by their score of successful matches. Each one of these bureaus boasts of their 'hits' – the marriages cemented through their offices. That is the ultimate criterion of success and forms their tagline. According to newspaper reports, marriage bureaus often boast about the amount of money spent on the marriages they have arranged, with some figures going as high as 100 crores or more. The brokers claim that they are happy to be rendering a social service. When a journalist asked an 'elite' matchmaker, 'And what are your rich clients looking for?', pat came the reply, 'Wealth!' To marry into wealth is the means of pursuing an ideal lifestyle, where brandishing brand names is a conscious assertion of shouting, 'Look I have money!' Apart from wealth, 'high status' commands a huge premium in the marriage market. As author Pavan Varma points out: 'Indians accord a high premium to acquiring status ... Nothing reveals the obsession with status more dramatically than the matrimonial ads in Indian newspapers.'[12] In an analysis undertaken of the matrimonial column in the *Times of India*, the phrase 'high status' is mentioned in as many as 1,532 advertisements. A magazine article on the subject of marriage highlights the role of the broker along these lines: Brokers sagely advise parents to get their daughters registered by the age of 22 or so. 'And why?' if a parent queries in utter bewilderment at the prospect of having their girls registered so young, the answers reek of a mindset firmly embedded in the Victorian age. A woman's greatest qualification is centered on her beauty and so the broker responds, 'because women lose the freshness of their looks after this, best to get them married as early as possible.'

For a parent to go through the process of finding a match for one's child, especially daughters, is an exercise in embracing one of the great lessons of Vedanta – the jettisoning of the ego. It is manifested in every medium where the bride's parents advertise for a suitable match, and the power equations get established right away.

Nitha Kumar, a doctor in her fifties, after having exhausted other options in finding a match for her 28-year-old daughter, who too is a doctor, decided to brave the portals of a marriage bureau in New Delhi. Nitha had imagined that she was going to expert professionals, who would help her in her quest. Instead she recalls her experience as a montage aimed at the reduction of the self. The fusillade of questions from the man behind the registration desk, asked with little sensitivity or finesse were meant to assess her and her family's net worth in terms of income, social circle, the number of holidays they took annually, in India or abroad, education, and finally the all-important question – how much will you spend on the wedding? This last one would determine the kind of match that the bureau would look for. As the bureau man concluded, 'Madam, the more ghee you pour, the better the taste of the food!' Later, when she was able to put some perspective to her discomfiture, she did admit that given the conditions, the questions served their purpose as the only method of ascertaining the 'eligibility criteria'.

A Suitable Bride

The image of a bride's parents doused with worry and anxiety until the girl's hands are smeared with haldi – a preparatory ritual before getting married – is deeply steeped in north Indian culture with endless references in popular songs, folk music and movies. In Telugu weddings too, the haldi ceremony called *pendlikoothuru* or *paindipilla* denotes the celebratory beginnings of a wedding, while in Tamil weddings we have the *mangala snaanam* where the groom and bride anointed with a mix of turmeric and *kumkum*, in their own homes, are readied for the vows. While traditionally the onus of fixing a daughter's wedding has been her father's preserve, the responsibility is now shared by the mothers too. Even present-day mothers, otherwise interested in looks and lifestyle, resort to some traditional processes to find a suitable boy. At the receiving end of an inexhaustible stream of unsolicited advice from older relatives and counselling from peer groups, the mother of a girl of marriageable age seems to exist in a parallel universe, where all her actions are geared towards a single goal, i.e. getting her daughter married. Ironically, her fate is a little like Austen's much spoofed character Mrs. Bennet in *Pride and Prejudice*, of whom the author adds caustically, 'the business of her life was to get her daughters married,' and who bemoaning her fate (of getting five daughters –with no fortunes, married) says, 'nobody is on my side ... I am cruelly used, nobody feels for my poor nerves...nobody can tell what I suffer!' Bollywood employs similar brushstrokes for such a character. In Rajkumar Hirani's popular film *Three Idiots*, there is a satirical depiction of the mother of one of the three protagonists. From a lower-income family, she has an emaciated physique and sunken eyes, burdened with the onerous responsibility of getting her daughter married. Her incessantly-articulated worries shared with her son adds to his unhappiness too. He attempts suicide, but falls into a coma instead. Lying comatose in a hospital ward, he is unmoved by the pleas, the chatter, the staged buffoonery, or the emotional promises made by his two friends. But when one of them, in a final bid to revive him, announces 'Your sister's match is fixed, that too without a dowry!' he is literally pulled out of the coma and in melodramatic happiness, opens his eyes.

How this view affects a woman's self-esteem or aid her in exploring career options, remains a moot point, when her worth is tied only to the marital status. Family members in a mixture of jest and anxiety often tell a woman of marriageable age, to quickly find a husband and depart to her 'real' home. The cultural precepts of this thought process are so pervasive that many girls see their single status as a time of waiting in the wings, as it were, before marriage.

The anxiety around a woman's marriage cuts across cultures, with many pejorative connotations attached to a woman who is spinsters of a certain age. Feminists have called it a 'particularly pernicious form of symbolic violence that marriage enacts on women in contemporary (western) societies [which] is the sense that they are flawed and failing if unmarried,' a pressure often built-up by popular media, films and in the Indian context, by the families.[13]

However, in recent times parents of sons in their late twenties or early thirties, are assailed by a similar rush of anxiety regarding the fate of their unmarried son and the fear of the tap running dry for prospective brides, as had traditionally been the preserve of the parents of daughters. The anxiety quotient is aggravated further if they think that their son is ready to 'settle down', a much-bandied term for getting married, presumably because the man has finished his education and is earning his living.

Things are changing for women too. Not all women are driven by the need to post their pictures on Facebook, as doe-eyed brides celebrating the triumphal march to matrimony. Many are busy pursuing life's other goals and are unfazed by the pressure of finding a partner. Forty-five-year-old Rita heads her own, very successful business. Work is the trigger that makes her life worthwhile. Divorced only after a couple of years of marriage, she finds men too intrusive and bossy, and doesn't wish to marry again. Brinda,* (name changed) now fifty, has never been married. She recently resigned from a senior position from an airline. With no financial compulsions, she lives happily with her mother. Supriya,* (name changed) nudging fifty, also doesn't wish to get married. She says her parents worry about her future after they've died. But she knows that her career, money in the bank and her network of friends, will sustain her. She has no wish to get married for financial compulsions, as she has seen some women do. 'Marriage is about economics too, and I have enough of my own, Thank Goddess!'

Matrimony and Technology – A Holy Embrace

While the conventional matchmaking avenues continue to be relevant, in the last decade or so, online matchmaking websites have really taken off in India. According to the last census (2011) there were 85 million urban Indians potentially looking for a match. Statista, the online market researcher, predicts that the online matrimonial sites earned around $13 million in 2018, with projections that at least half of the singles, approximately 41 million, would have gone online to find their matches or dates by the year 2022.[14] The base is growing like never before. Remember Shaadi.com, the first matrimonial website in India? Founded way back in 1996, it revolutionized the industry, shrewdly tapping into a market that has an insatiable love for technology and a deep, cultural imperative to find suitable partners for the eligible boy or girl in the family.[15] The company was the result of a business move, where its owner saw a huge vacuum in the wedding advertisement market. The traditional broker, constrained by time and geographical boundaries, would spend a day covering just about a couple of homes, while the market demanded hundreds and thousands of young women and men to have their proposals made accessible and vetted by prospective matches. By current estimates, Shaadi.com adds 10,000 new users a day, with an existing database of a whopping 20 million registrations! Nothing to validate success like the imitators brigade and so, following the success of Shaadi.com, a host of other websites jumped into the fray with names like Bharatmatrimony.com, Simplymarry.com, Jeevansathi.com. But when the broad-based matchmaking business shrank, portals turned to particular communities and sites like Tamilmatrimony.com, Brahminmatrimony.com, Sindhimatrimony.com.

Marketing compulsions have prompted these sites to evolve elaborate strategies to maximize their chances to hit the right profile. The registerant is advised to add a comprehensive biodata including a flattering photograph, which the site duly watermarks. 'Insufficient data' is apparently not conducive to hits. And so begins the road to successfully landing a possible life partner.

A demanding client base requires specialized strategies from these portals to accommodate their special profiles. Some entitled customers, feeling hemmed in by the limits of the general portals where the responses don't necessarily match their expectations, turn to high-end portals, such as Sycorian[16] and Indian Millionaire Marriages.com. These websites focus solely on super-wealthy customers, and have few qualms about telling the masses to keep away from their hallowed client base. Market experts claim that this elite market, worth approximately 100 crores and more, is crying to be tapped, making a compelling argument for more wedding sites catering to the elite. However, the online site is no guarantor for generating a great match, for while there may be enough success stories, there are countless misses before one makes that successful hit. The process of sifting through hundreds of profiles that these websites spew out almost with mechanical precision, demands endless hours of perusing, patience and perseverance, to finally zero in on the possibility of a prospect. As a young woman summed up, as she helped her mother go through hundreds of profiles looking for the elusive 'Mr. Right', 'You have to kiss a lot of frogs before you find Prince Charming.'

The rising popularity of online matrimonial sites gives us an understanding of how the country is adopting newer methods to scour for the right partner. But has modern technology wrought any changes to the matchmaking process, which has traditionally worked on meticulous compiling of class, caste, community, region and religion? Social scientists have posed several questions to assess if the internet has helped usher in the much-needed winds of change.[17,18] This could be a series of searching questions scripted possibly along these lines: has the agency of fixing the match shifted away from parents to the progeny? Are more of these marriages fixed according to one's personal choice? Are the resulting marriages more gender equal? Do changing ideas of courtship, intimacy and conjugal bliss make the internet the preferred mode?

The big shift initiated by the online matrimonial sites is that the youth have gained greater agency in choosing their partners. The change transpired not because parents willingly handed over the baton, but because manoeuvering the internet was quite puzzling for many of them. And so, the marrying individual found herself in the driver's seat negotiating the demands of matchmaking websites, with parents peering anxiously over their shoulders.

India certainly has impressive figures in internet usage. According to Statista, India will have some 635.8 million people using the internet by 2021, second only to China, with some 38 per cent of these belonging to the 24–35 age group.[19] The ease with which the young use the internet, only makes it easier for them to post their own profiles and monitor the responses. The smartphone is also a great way to get acquainted with a possible match, since a chat feature adds a nearly romantic sheen to the exercise. But where the internet matchmaker has failed to make a greater dent is in the strict divisions of gotra,[20] caste, community, etc. With the young leading the charge, one would have hoped that the list of qualifications would become more relaxed, but it seems that technology is now being employed to facilitate the traditional aspects of the matchmaking process as studies show. Even a quick visit to a marriage portal would allow one to see the lists of meticulously designed divisions of caste and sub-castes, compiled with an obsessive fussiness that would have done the family pandit proud. A long drop-down menu tells a prospective bride or groom about where they qualify in the caste stakes, followed by the standard education and status of the family. Some even have the horoscope-matching option, giving us an India where technology and tradition make a combustible combination.

And as for gender, the interweb lives up to its reputation of being dominated by men. Men post their profiles on their own, while a woman has a relative or a friend to post on her behalf, creating a buffer zone between her and the world of the prospective groom. Why don't women become their own agents? The answers all point in one direction – that it is the same cultural context that has put women behind in the digital revolution. According to various statistical sites just 30 per cent of women in India were online in 2018, though this has gone up by nearly 10 per cent in the following year.[21] So there's hope yet.

Patriarchal families seeking to control women's choices and sexuality frown upon a woman actively looking for a partner online. To add to this cultural baggage is the idea of modesty and feminine reticence, which women are indoctrinated into from a very young age. Though positive changes are happening with many more women speaking their minds about their expectations from a future husband, their numbers are way below men who come armed with a laundry list of the kind of women they wish to marry. Another impediment keeping women away from these websites is the disturbing prospect of encountering online predators.

But whatever process a family may choose to follow, cutting across all the heads of caste, class and community, most middle-class households would still give a premium to that vague qualification of 'good family'. The broker is pretty adept at deciphering the atomized composition of this term to mean a family where the folks will be good to their daughter-in-law, that she would be materially looked after and would score well on the 'happiness quotient'. Given this compulsion of getting a good family, it is equally important to project the worth of a prospective bride. And though technology has enabled a more user-friendly platform, the demands from the boy's and girl's side remain frozen in the parameters of a bygone era. The boys want beautiful, fair girls, sometimes with demands for a dowry, and sometimes 'demandless' i.e. no dowry. For the women, a good family and a husband earning well remain the top two qualifications. And so, gender inequalities have continued in the arranged marriage system.

Social Media as Cupid

'Love marriages', however, are changing some rules of the game. A part of this change has ridden on the back of the social media craze that has swept through the country, outstripping all other forms of communication in record time. India has some 270 million Facebook and Whatsapp users, outstripping USA by nearly a million. Those aged between 24–30 years continue to fuel its popularity, with an approximate 74 per cent usage cornered by men. According to a report by the Boston Consulting Group, rural consumers will constitute about half of India's internet users by 2020.[22] How do these colossal numbers affect our social behaviour? How have mobile phones affected romantic relationships? Another survey by a TV channel showed that while one out of three students claimed that they used the net for research work and thereby improved their grades, 67 per cent youth admitted to the obvious – they used mobiles for reaching out to their friends.[23] For the youth the great joy of using the internet to communicate with friends is that parents can't fully control who they are texting or talking to. While the landline phones replaced written love letters with long phone calls whispering sweet-nothings, oddly enough, mobile phones have revived written communication via e-mails and texting.

While the last decade saw India's youth gravitating towards social media as a novel communicating tool, jettisoning voice calls almost as an anachronism in the process, contemporary times have seen technology being put to ever more astonishing usage. The growing popularity of mobile-only apps, incorporating AI (artificial intelligence) to facilitate uniquely individualistic experiences on the various platforms, where the medium is but an extension of one's creativity and imagination, aided of course by rapidly accessible smartphones and data usage, has seen the millennial generation employ ever more innovative ways for their romantic ideas to fly.

Social media has given the youth the tools to connect with friends insulated from the snoopy intrusiveness of elders, which was unavoidable in previous generations. It's therefore unsurprising that those wanting to keep an omniscient presence in their children's lives are deeply suspicious of this medium. There are countless instances where whole communities have tried to ban young unmarried girls from using mobiles, trumpeting a variety of reasons, from alleging that it distracts them from their studies to getting into 'bad situations' where they learn to elope.[24]

However, love marriages, are increasingly becoming the norm in urban, middle-income families, where parents without a trace of self-consciousness say that they would be happy if their children could find their own partners and relieve them of the burden of matchmaking. Some parents are even heard bemoaning the fact that their daughter/son just cannot seem to find anybody, and now they have been burdened by that task. On the other end of the spectrum are the more conservative families, where the choice of partner for a child remains very much the family's preserve. They declare in emphatic terms that they will not allow any violation of that covenant. Some want their sons married to relieve the mother's loneliness, as her grown-up children don't want her constant nurturing anymore robbing her of her purpose in life, or some need a daughter-in-law to look after the household and care for them in their old age. The matchmaking process is not fully focused on the young, it must factor in parental needs as well. This is particularly so for a son and his wife; the arrangement works entirely differently for the daughter, whose loyalties are co-opted by her husband's home.

Arranged Marriage vs Love Marriage

Arranged or Love, which is better? This question often fires the imagination of the youth, even as social scientists try to understand the Indian marriage scenario from this particular point of view. Success in a marriage is gauged from vastly different viewpoints by different people. The arranged wedding is solemnized with the central concept that the couple will travel the journey from their youth to their old age, fulfilling the duties of the householder; notions of romantic love, intellectual compatibility or personal fulfillment rarely, if ever, form a part of the process of matchmaking. While the love marriage is based on the idea of a romantic attraction for the other as its fundamental core. This clear focus on negotiating a journey, pitfalls and all, is part of the *saptapadi* that the couples exchange. While this may echo some of the sentiments exchanged by the couple in a typical church wedding – 'to have and to hold from this day forward, for better, for worse, for richer, for poorer, in sickness and in health, to love and to cherish, till death us do part, according to God's holy law' – yet there are crucial differences. The Hindu marriage is typically seen as a sacrament according to the Manusmriti and the Vedas, where the woman and man are together for several lifetimes. These traditional beliefs have had more earthly interventions through laws such as the Hindu Marriage Act, 1955 and its Amendment Act, 1976 bringing dramatic changes that have removed some of the sacramental nature of Hindu marriage as a lifelong bond or one that travels beyond life. Yet the imprint remains, and marriage as a partnership through the lifecycles is embedded within belief systems. Perhaps this is one explanation for the low divorce rates in India with just about 1 per cent of marriages going to the courts according to a report by the

Organisation for Economic Co-operation & Development from 2017. This is remarkable considering that by western standards, young couples, particularly the women, have their lives ordered according to the strictures of their elders. Separations are a more regular occurrence, but often reconciliations remain a part of the arrangements with interventions by older members, both expected and fairly commonplace in such scenarios. While it could be certainly argued that low economic status does hinder women from ending their relationship with an incompatible partner, as argued elsewhere, the connection of a union over several births, continues to be reinforced by rituals, ornamental symbols of one's marriage and various kinds of fasts which aim at prolonging the husband's life.

While arranged marriages largely follow certain set precepts, the eligibility list seems to be under some pressure of late. It's not unusual to have women marrying men who are younger or shorter or with a lower income. Exposure to a globalized world is ushering in this attitudinal shift amongst the urban youth and is most visible in those who have migrated from their hometowns with all its accompanying restrictions on social behaviour and 'what will people say!' chastity belts.

An Arranged Love Marriage

The Indian matrimonial narrative, as numerous surveys have shown, favours the arranged marriage system. This promises a certain familiarity of arrangements that at a deeper level perpetuates the concept of caste and gender roles. By contrast, love marriages defying parental approval are disruptive, questioning the set notions of marriage patterns. An interesting development has occurred between these polarities, which accommodates the traditional roles of the family and youthful aspirations of romantic love. This is the 'arranged love' marriage, which is gaining immense traction across the country. Here a couple is brought together by parents or professional matchmakers. Once the vetting is done and approvals granted, the boy and the girl are allowed to get to know each other better and take some time to interact on their own. There are also increasing instances where marriages are arranged flouting the boundaries of caste and community. The focus in these cases shifts to what in urban parlance is termed 'compatibility'. The tick marks are now sought against a different set of requirements such as education, looks, job, club memberships, a good address, and so forth. Marriages might be made in heaven or in algorithms, but the tremendous variable between a yes or a no – the governor of future happiness, the determiner of destiny – lies in those nano-seconds when two, free-thinking adults are poised to decide. This augurs a process of social churning that has the potential of rearranging the rigidly subscribed social systems as we have known them. The rumblings are clearly discernible, but the impact and breadth of this change is a story that shall be scripted in the future.

3

WEDDINGS AND THE KISS OF MONEY

The 'Big Fat Indian Wedding' has of late become a collective adjective for an increasingly elaborate event, fat on moolah, magnificent in scale and meticulously insulated from a world beleaguered by the tyranny of cutbacks and shrinking economies. A wedding these days is a fantasy of romance and the good life, and the world – i.e. one's family, friends and acquaintances – is invited to witness a movie-like production of the celebrations. For the young woman or man, ready to take the big step, it is a watershed event, marking the crossover from student life to the adult world. For parents, it is another major milestone in their life's journey – from their own youth to now getting their child married.

What makes weddings so special for Indian families bound by traditional cultural mores? The answer, for such a religiously oriented country, can be found in its scriptural trove and its pantheon of gods and goddesses. While many religions see the wedding as a marker of fertility rites or a divinely sanctioned union, in many Hindu communities, the wedding is the earthly enactment of the union of the divine couple – Shiva and Parvati,[1] with the bride and groom stepping briefly into divinely ordained roles. There are of course some regional variations. In the Tamil wedding for instance the groom briefly takes on the avatar of Lord Vishnu and the parents of the bride accord him special honour in that role, with the father of the bride washing his feet during the Pada Puja ceremony. This fusion of religion and tradition, topped with a generous dose of family participation, makes it, for most Indians, the mother of all celebrations.

The Economics of the Rich and Famous

India's economic boom have transformed weddings into statement shows that celebrate the potent mix of love and money. And into this trove of wealth and good times, arrived the NRIs – propelled by nostalgia, Bollywood and a weakening rupee, marking their weddings as lavish, extraordinary revisits in the family album.

In 2015, the British-Indian billionaire Sanjay Hinduja got married in Udaipur in a grandiose event spread over multiple days, and the tabloids couldn't get enough of it. 'My big fat £15 MILLION wedding!' read the headline in the *Daily Mail* as it covered all the details on the celebrity guests, the number of chartered planes that ferried their 16,000 guests and how much the rooms cost.[2]

Cut to 2019 and the excessive quotient reaches stratospheric heights. The Ambani weddings are the new gold standard for being the most extravagant and opulent of them all. Mukesh Ambani, Asia's richest man and amongst the top 20 wealthiest people in the world, threw two splashy weddings for his children Isha and Akash within months of each other. Social media braced itself to the task, sending carefully scripted vignettes of the event to millions of smartphones. From a ₹3,00,000 wedding invitation to pre-nuptial events where their mother Nita Ambani looking like a Bollywood diva was dancing on lavish sets – the excessive fairy tale was played and replayed on people's phones. The first of these weddings – the fantastical world conjured by the Ambanis and Piramals – was attended by the first families of Bollywood like the Bachchans, the Khans, Deepika Padukone, Ranveer Singh, Rajnikanth etc. Also in attendance were the former US Secretary of State Hillary Clinton, former President Pranab Mukherjee and Sachin Tendulkar. But underlying the endless theatrics, was the image of the bride Isha, swathed in wealth and the groom Ajay, an industrial scion from one of India's oldest business families, taking the *saptapadi* around the sacred fire. The powerful emotional quotient provided by other visuals – of Nita invoking the blessing of the gods and Mukesh wiping his tears at his daughter's *vidaai*, or leaving for her in-laws' – tugged at the heartstrings of millions around the country. A breathless media filed every tiny detail of the magnum opus – from the designers and make-up artists to who danced with whom. There was the story of Beyoncé coming to Udaipur to perform at Isha's sangeet, at the end of which she reportedly presented a $4 million bill. But through all the peripheral optics the grapevine remained firmly centered around speculating what the wedding had actually cost. By some estimates it was a $100 million and others whittled it down to ₹100 crores.[3] *LA Times* summed it up with, 'The Ambani nuptials have set a new standard for over-the-top opulence – a mark of the oligarchs who have become unimaginably wealthy in India's three-decade rise from a sleepy quasi-socialist state to one of the world's fastest-growing major economies.'[4]

So what does ₹100 crores really mean? To give scale to the figure, let's look at the Indian government's budgets. In 2014, the government had allotted ₹6,020 crores to develop 100 smart cities, the package included developing modern and efficient infrastructure. It means that the government was allotting approximately ₹100 crores each year towards developing each city over a period of 5 years. The money would look at 'invigorating urban renewal for its 30 per cent population and create engines of growth that would fuel the survival of the remaining 70 per cent spread across over 5,00,000 hamlets and villages.'[5] In effect, ₹100 crores a year would be deployed to affect millions of human beings, so they could have their share of the country's resources and live with dignity. Such a quantum jump in possibilities is imagined through the spending of the same amounts of money that was spent on one wedding over some seven days of celebrations. A big wedding is not merely confined to big money but is about making a statement – the bigger, the better. And it is a truly successful event when the media churns out screaming headlines about the smallest details and personal videos shot by the guests go viral. It's with such impulses that the uber rich set out to create the wedding of the year, year after year.

The weddings of the rich and famous provide endless fodder for the insatiable public. The cost of the outfits, their designers, the guest list, the food, the decor, the gifts, the honeymoon – all of this is regurgitated by the media, which the obliging public laps up eagerly. And so, barely was the Ambani wedding over, that the public was inundated with fascinating glimpses into actress Priyanka Chopra's wedding with the Hollywood star Nick Jonas. Once again the tabloids and fashion magazines told us what Chopra wore for her bridal shower, and how Ralph Lauren, who never made wedding dresses other than the three for his own family, actually made one for Priyanka, and how many thousands of hours went into the making of her Indian wedding dress.[6]

This abiding fascination with the rich and famous is probably a human instinct rooted in our past when the weddings of kings and queens unfolded like spectator sports for their fawning subjects. Till date, we are enthralled by the spectacular show of Lady Diana and Prince Charles's wedding or a generation later, of Prince William and Kate, or closer home, Bollywood royalty Deepika Padukone and Ranveer Singh's wedding – their stories fulfilling our need to objectify the exalted, the rich and the celebrated.

India's Long Tradition of Big Weddings

India's wedding celebrations are part of a long tradition. In the past, royal families have conducted their weddings in style, beautifully preserved by artists in miniature paintings, sculptures, historical documents and royal artefacts, that pay tribute to the extravagance and grand imagination of these weddings. Even early twentieth century royal weddings, held under the colonial sway, weren't lacking in pomp and splendour. A YouTube video of the Maharaja of Patiala's wedding held in 1933, showcases an astounding grandeur, with untold wealth at his disposal, ensconced as the princely kingdom was under the benign eye of the English ruling class. Zamindars (land-owners) were next in the hierarchy, followed by the rich trader classes who, by the middle of the twentieth century had accumulated enough wealth to emulate their superior classes in their own weddings.

Weddings earned their grand status by the number of guests in attendance or the unusually expensive gifts given to the girl. One of my ancestral relatives had once been given a silver embellished bed – a gift so ludicrously extravagant that it has become an exotic anecdote in our family history. Today, grand weddings aren't restricted to the royalty. Or perhaps the royals have been replaced by industrialists, movie stars, sports heroes and the political classes.

The NRI Wedding that Set the Trend

The trend of the big NRI wedding is largely credited to L.N. Mittal, the UK-based steel magnate whose son got married in Calcutta in 1998. The media went into a frenzy since a wedding of that scale had not lent its glamour quotient to the city in contemporary times. The pathbreaking décor, the sensational sangeet, held in the Victoria Memorial grounds (that imposing legacy of the Raj), a glamorous guest list packed with Bollywood stars – it created a virtual storm as one of India's big weddings of the time. The steel tycoon introduced a magnificence of scale that was still unprecedented in circles outside of the royal families or film stars. In his dismissal of the prevailing practice of modesty and restraint that marked the weddings of the wealthy of Calcutta (largely belonging to Mittal's own community, the Marwaris), he fused wealth and imagination to replicate global standards for celebrity weddings. That grand wedding stoked an inherent love among people to celebrate weddings as a tamasha. It coincided with the time when the country was riding the crest of an economic wave, which brought unparalleled wealth to a section of its people and gave rise to a wealthy middle-class that wanted more of everything, a sentiment captured by the famous Pepsi slogan of the late 1990s, '*Ye Dil Maange More*'.[7]

This newly-acquired wealth poured into the wedding market, which expanded exponentially within a short time to cope with the demand. The number of big-ticket weddings began to spiral. An editor for a foreign publication shared his stupefied wonderment at the scale of these extravaganzas, 'Each year, around

2,000 high-end weddings take place in India. These are multi-day extravaganzas that defy the Western imagination, complete with pyrotechnics, performances by gyrating Bollywood actors and international music stars, and thousands upon thousands of invited guests.'[8]

In 2011, the politician Kunwar Singh Tanwar spent ₹250 crore on his son's wedding. Though this time the blogs and gossip columns were tinged with a censorious air. It was difficult to ignore the profligacy fuelling the wedding, the unexplained reservoirs of wealth of a public servant.[9]

Weddings and Fashion Trends

Traditionally, the wealthy in India have equated luxury goods with jewellery, watches, cars, writing instruments, antiques and art. These then became family keepsakes, handed over to the next generation. Clothes didn't qualify as an investment and were therefore allotted more modest budgets. In that era of financial conservativeness, men could wear a Western suit or a shervani stitched by the local tailor for special occasions. The women were more stylish and favoured chiffon saris – French chiffons for the very wealthy – and kanjeevarams, jamawars and pashmina shawls. The middle-class income groups, driven by the more pragmatic compulsions of saving for a daughter's trousseau, bought gold and silver as their version of the luxury splurge.

However, in the post-liberalization period Indians have embraced luxury like an oasis for desert travellers. Media frenzy has also brought in an unprecedented need to locate evermore exotic venues, and subsequently construct them into fantasy visions of luxury, harnessing an assemblage of designers and experts. Buying brands is definitely an aspirational exercise, and the push for luxury goods remains overwhelmingly driven by a wedding-oriented market. As fashion designer Tarun Tahiliani puts it, 'People don't dress up for the day at all ... they only dress up to go to parties or to weddings — and the wedding is the big thing ... It encompasses the black-tie event, the museum opening, the gala benefit all in one. All of the things that people would wear couture or evening gowns to abroad, only happens around the wedding. There is nothing else [that compares].'

Weddings are fuelling the couture market, that promises huge dividends not just for celebrity fashion designers, but even for those outside the marquee billing, as Sabyasachi Mukherjee, one of India's most prolific designers remarked, since fashion has a trickle-down effect.[10] This includes the vast ocean of India's tailoring and stitching talent – which encompasses young designers, neighbourhood boutiques, the local *darzee*, home-based tailors – all of whom immerse themselves into catering to the voracious hunger of the wedding market. While highly competitive and lucrative, this market is unfortunately a hotbed of unimaginative inspiration. Trickling down from the rarefied quarters of the designer world are the imitations, the adaptations, the cheap mock-ups of the sartorial inspirations seen on the ramps. They form a rough template for the thousands of wedding lehengas and outfits displayed on buxom mannequins in shops lined along the dingy lanes and bylanes of the country's cities and towns, whether it be Lucknow, Hyderabad or Kolkata.

Weddings in movies and on soap operas too inspire the wedding look. In the movie *Kuch Kuch Hota Hai*, Kajol wore the three-piece hair accessory, the *bena bandhi* traditionally worn in UP and Bihar, to complete her bridal look. This became so trendy that aspiring brides searched through jewellery shops to get the same look. Deepika Padukone wore traditional Banarasi in her various wedding outfits, giving the fabric a contemporary makeover that spells high fashion. It also brought a much-needed revival for the weavers, who were moving away from the traditional crafts for the lack of patronage.

Wedding Economics

The exponential increase in wedding budgets has caught the attention of global players and industrial houses. They want to understand, as in this survey by Kotak, the spending patterns of the super rich, whose net worth hovers around ₹250 crores and above, with the total net worth of high net-worth individuals expected to touch ₹352 trillion by 2022.[11] Luxury brands have caught the imagination of these classes and so it is predicted that the luxury segment will grow to an approximately ₹3.5 lakh crore market in the next couple of years.[12]

Luxury, for the super rich, is not merely about brands, but about possessing the rare one-of-a-kind piece, a whim that drives outlandish purchases such as a set of emerald earrings costing ₹1 crore or a handbag that outstrips the cost of a luxury car. These goods are props to announce that one has arrived. As Ankit Malhotra, CEO of Comme Sogne Vero, a high-end wedding planning company in Delhi, says with delicious humour about the famously aspirational levels of a certain section of the city's rich, desperate to copy the Joneses', in this case the South Delhi crowd, by using their weddings as vehicles to announce their arrival in the wealth stakes. He adds that everyone has a certain budget, but destination weddings seem to have no upper limit. Whether Bali or Thailand or Goa or Udaipur, these weddings are about some make-believe fantasy, and no expense is spared to complete the feeling. He gives an example of a South Delhi socialite of great wealth and taste. She wanted to make sure that her daughter's destination wedding was perfect. And to do that she made ten visits to Bali to plan it right.

Adorning the Bride

The big splurge these days is the jewellery, where investments have reached stratospheric levels. An upper-class bride has several looks depending on the number of functions, and every designer outfit is matched with a different set of jewellery – rubies and emeralds, chunky solitaires and polki (rough-cut diamonds) – all befitting the bride's trousseau. But it's the shiny yellow metal that dominates the Indian imagination and has the lion's share of the jewellery market. A mindboggling 400 tonnes of gold is exchanged at weddings each year in the country, and it is the single biggest expenditure in Indian weddings, worth around ₹1.25 lakh crores a year. Gold continues to be that most precious part of the trousseau or *streedhan* given to the daughter for her wedding. While a new wave of gender discourse argues in favour of bequeathing property to the daughter, which the courts have endorsed by way of the Hindu Succession (Amendment) Act, 2005, deep-seated prejudices remain.[13] Instead, most middle-class families give gold and other jewellery at their daughter's wedding as her share of the family wealth, whose value only increases in time. Gold has historically been deeply entwined with an Indian woman's sense of wealth and importantly, auspiciousness – an intricate mix of beauty, womanhood and familial and religious blessings. The metal though has caused a class divide, with the upper classes showing a clear preference for diamonds and polki over gold. But across the spectrum, families still repose their faith in gold, collecting it assiduously over the years for their daughter's wedding, safekeeping those gold bangles to pass on as family heirlooms, and if things take a nosedive financially, to redeem it and renew the family coffers.

Wedding Designs

Big weddings have set sky-high aspirations in the hearts and minds of betrothed couples and their parents, irrespective of their budget. The buildup has become an elaborate directory of functions and non-events that are made momentous with generous doses of grandeur, all of which is designed to peak like a star performer's final surge, in the magnificence of the wedding. And so the functions – the bachelorette, the bridal shower, the sundowner, the mehendi, the cocktails, the haldi, the sangeet, each with its own theme, go on and on until the wedding itself. The director of the show i.e. the wedding planner, has a finger on every pulse of every ceremony, their minute instructions bellowing on walkie-talkies buzzing amongst the floral designer, the set designer, the caterer, the Michelin-starred chef, the DJ, the decorator, the carriage bearer, the transport coordinator, etc. The moniker 'wedding planner' is a recent creation that became hugely popular in the wake of the popular movie *Band Baaja Baaraat* released in 2010. The stars of the movie Ranveer Singh and Anushka Sharma, gave a glimpse of what professional wedding planners can do to the look and smooth organization of a wedding. The 2019 web series *Made in Heaven* has perfectly depicted a wedding planner's role as the wedding *sutradhar*, the eyes and ears of the wedding who sometimes doubles up as the agony aunt. She also plays the big, if unwanted, role of the crisis manager.

Ratna Chadha, the chairperson of Tirun Travels, that organizes luxury cruises, shuddered impressively when asked about one of her most challenging moments of organizing a wedding on board. 'This whole baraat was to fly in from Kolkata in the morning,' she recounts. 'Enough time to catch the cruiser from Singapore, no question about that. So we were all relaxed. But as luck would have it the Air India flight that day was delayed by eight hours. It seemed that the whole wedding plan was going to go for a toss. The ship would have sailed according to schedule, four hours before the wedding party arrived. We thought this was it! No shaadi-vaadi on the ship. All that money gone down the tube. Everyone was panicky. And to top it all, the bride's mother kept calling me from Singapore, as if she was on auto call – every ten minutes at least. 'What's happening?' Do this, do that... so many suggestions, and here I was feeling so helpless. Thankfully, the airline managed another aircraft and we could arrive in time for the ship. I can tell you, never again do I want to have a repeat of that tension!' she ends with another expressive shudder.

The Countdown Begins

The wedding has traditionally been featured as a big event in the family calendar, but it is only in the last couple of decades that fresh interpretations backed with money and aspirations have scaled them to such ambitious levels. The contrast to how weddings panned out just a couple of decades back to the blockbuster extravaganzas of today, is a telling comment on a changing India. It would not be amiss to walk down those sepia-tinted lanes of yore in order to get a measure of how much has changed.

But first a contemporary cameo. Green buntings fluttering in the salubrious Goa air cast angular shadows on the waters of the hotel swimming pool. The air pulsates to the tune of a mashup version of 'mehendi laga ke rakhna', the DJ has turned on an irresistible beat, the crowd on its feet. Further away sat groups of women, some with their arms extended as the mehendi-walis drew patterns of green on their palms. In their midst, sat the beautiful bride, whose palms and feet were being skilfully and painstakingly covered with intricate designs of fresh henna, that would take hours to dry before its dark red could stain her skin. Servers were carrying around trays of snacks and drinks, with straws for women with mehendi on their hands. This was the mehendi function – an auspicious and core element of the bride's elaborate beauty regimen. This was now a key ceremony amongst the host of functions that build up to the wedding. But it was not always so.

A few decades back, the mehendi was a nondescript affair – a basic pattern on the palms, daubed with some expertise by a relative or a neighbour. Amongst some Hindu communities the henna didn't feature at all, and instead *alta*, a washable red dye, was used to colour a girl's hands and feet that proclaimed her bridal status. As with the henna, the bride's makeup too was a quiet homely affair. It would start with the preparatory ritual of using a herbal body polisher or *ubtan* – a beauty secret handed down from the grandmothers. An older sister or female relative with a nodding acquaintance with cosmetics, was roped in to put on the lipstick, kajal and powder, which formed the modest beauty kits of the time.

This scenario has changed drastically. Nowadays, the bride's mehendi, which is central to this function, takes hours to get done, and there is music and dancing and lunch and parting gifts for the guests to complete the celebration. Hair and makeup is done by professional beauticians, whose reputation is closely scrutinized before she can use her skills on the bride. The head beautician brings her team. Professional to the core, there are specialized hair stylists, makeup artists, the saree-draper who does the lehenga and the chunri, and a bevy of helpers, so that while the bride gets top priority, a few chosen relatives too get professional help. All of this comes at a price, of course.

The bride, who is central to the whole exercise, has been transformed from her earlier avatar, the archetypal image of bridal coyness – silent, demure, with downcast eyes – an image impressed on our collective imaginations through countless such portrayals in Indian films and popular media. Her involvement kept to a minimum in the arrangements, she was in many ways a woman without agency, much like the bridegroom, with both the key players enjoined to enact an expected puppet-like role at the command of elders and the pandit.

Contemporary weddings follow a blueprint that is usually laid out by the bride, with some input from the groom. But the roles are fraught with their own set of challenges, exacerbated undoubtedly by the power dynamics between the bride and the bridegroom's side, with the latter invested with a certain veto power. In the choice of venue, detailing of ceremonies, the exchange of gifts, and the *khatirdari* or the hospitality extended to the groom's side, the bride's family is situated to appease the latter. In such situations, a bride, juggling the twin roles of a daughter negotiating the complex power play between the two sides, while acutely aware of her status as soon-to-be wife has to do some really tough tightrope walking. A particularly insightful beautician from a leading beauty parlour in Goa had this to say about young women: 'Brides are extremely stressed out. Often the constant demands from the boy's side have the mother and daughter lunging at each other, nerves tautened to snapping point and when they arrive at the parlour preparing finally for the Big Day, it's as if that mounting dam of tension reaches breaking point. We have had the most ugly battles between mothers and daughters right here in this parlour.' And so, we have brides venting their tension, while the mothers almost with Machiavellian wisdom will advise, 'You will have your say once you get married. Just go with the flow for now, you will have your moment.' This advice given to a young woman stepping into marriage, opens an interesting dimension into India's rising aspirations struggling against regressive gender roles and attitudes.

Today, the lines between the metropolises and provincial India are blurring. As the fascination for big weddings sweep across the country, every mofussil town is seeing wedding halls and wedding venues proliferating like memes. They also run to a type, projecting in many ways the middle-class vision of opulence, much like the building blocks that define luxury housing. Garishly mounted with statues of *apsaras* and sundry auspicious figures like elephants and horses in gold and silver, grand entrances festooned with fake flowers, fountains inspired from Vrindavan gardens and lines of tables for the buffet dinners catering to a thousand guests or so – they are designed to impress, however kitschy their execution.

In the metros, the venue costs alone carry a hefty tag of ₹10 lakhs and above. What is astounding is that even in the smaller towns, people no longer blanch when ludicrous figures are quoted. A relative of mine, who was organizing a wedding in Gwalior, a small town in Madhya Pradesh, hired a wedding venue for the princely sum of ₹7 lakhs. A cantonment town during the British era, Jhansi has a few industries even today, but its more wealthy population now aspires to hold their weddings in the five-star hotels in the tourist haven of Orchha some 18 kms away.

Consumption of wedding related goods has also spiked in these smaller towns. This has brought international brands, designer clothes and accessories manufacturers fast trotting to these smaller towns for periodic promotions, exhibitions, fairs and expos. A brand promoter for an international luxury brand of cosmetics talked about how the most impressive sales figures come in from towns like Indore and Coimbatore, where they could sell ₹6 lakhs worth of cosmetics in a single day, and a city like Kolkata in contrast would fetch them sales figures that were just about half the amount. The unmarried girls ready to make their debuts in the marriage market are sold on the seductive dream of using certain cosmetics. The pharmaceutical industry too reaps its bonanza from sundry skin creams, hair serums and whitening lotions, which have flooded shelf space in medical shops everywhere.

The exposure to a larger world and a culture that prioritizes personal appearance has also driven men to seek professional help for their looks. Gyms, attuned to the macho image, have been popular with men for a long time, but the march towards slimming clinics, skin clinics and spas is relatively new. An owner of a VLCC-franchised salon in the town of Gorakhpur in Uttar Pradesh, was taken aback by the sheer number of men who come to her clinic. In a way, a new gender identity is being written, as even those who see themselves as 'real men' want to get beautified for their big day. As with the women, it's not just the groom but all his male relatives and friends who want to live up to a starry image of macho good looks.

The lower end of the lower-middle-class – the drivers, peons, domestic help, nurses, and other small-time tradespeople too are evaluating themselves on the aspiration index. Peer pressure and the natural desire to up one's status is driving them to take steps that would help them gain middle-class respectability. Households, which are otherwise stretched to make ends meet, put everything together to throw lavish weddings. The bride gets dressed in a beauty parlour, her outfit embellished in the gold *zari* of a traditional Banarasi sari, the gold around her neck eliciting envious sighs from the onlookers. The bridegroom too arrives in a flower-bedecked car, a newly acquired suit proclaiming his enhanced status. The boy-wallah–girl-wallah divide is in operation here as well, with the bride's family paying for a large part of the expenses. 'The bride-wallahs don't have the *himmat* (courage) to ask the groom's side how much of the tab they will pick up, they are just too scared to ask. Even in a love marriage, the divide is very much there,' shares a wedding planner. 'Though today at least in 80 per cent cases, the groom's side does pay for an expensive function like the sangeet.'

Financing the Dream

But how do these desires sit with financial realities? For those whose purses have become fatter, the big wedding is a new opportunity for showing their wealth. But for those perennially challenged for money, meeting such expenses calls for innovative practices. India's inventiveness, its jugaad, comes to the rescue of the poor who have little access to organized loans. The first is to approach the networks of relatives, programmed along the lines of kin and mutual give and take. But this method, fraught with uncertainties and family politics is not entirely reliable. Next, one pleads with the employer and if that doesn't fructify, then the borrower has no recourse but to take a loan from the market, paying astronomical compound rates of interest. In urban centres, there is the rising popularity of the chit fund, referred to as the 'Committee'. An ingenious form of saving based on mutual trust as many people are involved in the transactions, it helps in meeting larger expenses, though it has a notorious history of being labeled a Ponzi scheme, with several promoters absconding with the kitty, as in the Saradha scam.[14]

Another way of raising wedding funds, is through selling of the family-owned land. Often done to meet a daughter's wedding expenses and her dowry, this can have a catastrophic effect on a family's fortunes. As every study on Indian weddings points out, grand visions of a wedding in reality puts huge pressure on the lives and budgets of the poor.[15] In contrast, wealthier families have the luxury of much larger reserves of wealth. Indians have always believed in spending far beyond their means for their child's wedding, so what is happening today is just a scale up.

The elephant in the room here is the unimaginably massive parallel economy or the 'black market', which looms colossus-like over the country's economy. It could be as high as 60 per cent of the GDP or ₹93 lakh crore,[16] and these unaccounted for fund high-end weddings. As one of India's leading designers Rohit Bal said in an interview, 'A lot of our clients have got so much undeclared wealth, where else will they spend it?'

Those in the luxury trade point out that the average Indian spends a staggering one-fifth of the wealth accumulated in his/her lifetime on a son or daughter's wedding, second only to investing in the family home. [17] This is reflective of Indian priorities, where a roof over one's head only mildly edges out the child's wedding as the top expense in a person's life.

Why the Big Wedding?

Reams have been written about how Indians love big weddings. Even though this whole fantasy buildup against the grim reality of the daily life of an average Indian family strikes a very discordant note. Several studies have been done to understand the psychology behind the phenomena, and though there are no clear answers, there are various theories that give us a glimpse of the psychology behind it.

Some eminent sociologists conducted a study to understand how the functioning of a particular society, moulds the manner in which a person behaves or spends.[17] Their study, though focused on a rural community, could apply equally well to an urban setting. Researchers show that 'wedding celebrations have a lot to do with social status and prestige. So, whether it's a small-time businessman in rural India or the multi-billionaire in Mumbai, the social compulsions have a familiar ring that beats location or class.'

To quote from a comprehensive anthology on India, 'In India there is no greater event in a family than a wedding, dramatically evoking every possible social obligation, kinship bond, traditional value, impassioned sentiment, and economic resource. In the arranging and conducting of weddings, the complex permutations of Indian social systems best display themselves. Marriage alliances entail some redistribution of wealth as well as building and restructuring social realignments.'[18]

For Indians who have lived largely in joint families, individuality has a very different meaning. For them, it is also about what their relatives have achieved. This, through a strange process of reverse osmosis, gives them a sense of accomplishment as well, leading to occasions where someone, when asked about their achievements, will invariably also talk about what their uncle, grandmother or cousin has achieved. This linking with relatives and transmitting their achievements and wealth to oneself, even though oblique sometimes, is integrated into the matchmaking process too. Prospective candidates often get long letters listing a detailed resume of the relatives with their achievements, present position, etc. from the proposing family.

The idea behind this shifting of focus from the self to a distant relative could perhaps be rooted in the inordinate pride that Indians take in ties of family and kinship. This is actually another way of announcing that one is well-connected and thus, deserves similar stature and respect.

Mobility within a village is often achieved by imitating the behaviours of families of the higher social orders, say some sociologists, and it is a value in itself.[19] The practice of marrying within one's caste and community is still the biggest reason why people spend beyond their capacity. In the end, those admiring and enduring gasps are truly worth the money spent for the man who has nearly emptied his bank account and is in debt. His rationale is located in a sense of honour within the community, and the size and scale of weddings is directly connected to this sentiment.

This idea of one's status in the community, is perhaps the prime motivator behind some big weddings in the country. As sociologists point out through their studies, a wedding is not a fairy tale where two people fall in love and say they are happy to live together ever after. In India it is overwhelmingly laden with some significant baggage, and social and cultural constructs. 'For the parents of a daughter, marriage is potentially the most important source of mobility since marrying into a "good family" can greatly enhance how a family is viewed by its peers, and a prestigious match is an occasion for great celebration and status displays. This, more than anything, explains why some weddings are particularly lavish.'[20] [21]

What Do the Millennials Want?

Today's Gen Z is no longer interested in the traditions that they have heard ad nauseum from their elders. Today's youth, weaned on a liberal, more Westernized lifestyle, has moved away from the family cocoons that the generation before them had been sequestered in.

A matchmaking service conducted an online survey to understand the different aspects of the Big Fat Indian Wedding. Its nearly 8,714 responses from singles and parents alike had as many as 57 per cent of young singles declaring that they aspired to have a destination wedding.[22] According to another estimate the Indian destination wedding industry would have a market size of ₹45,000 crores by 2020, with the annual growth going at 25–30 per cent. The factors stoking it are rising incomes, aspirations and the booming social media. Perhaps it may be a while yet before we see Indian couples doing what newlywed Japanese couples are doing – traipsing around the world with a photographer in tow for their wedding shoot, but the day doesn't seem too far off.

My own survey with approximately forty young people across middle-income groups in Kolkata and Delhi, shows that though many young women and men say they want a small wedding with just friends around them, they also want to obey their parents' wishes. It means they will acquiesce to the big wedding, where showing the guests a good time is the central objective, the ceremonies and peripheral traditions being add-ons. Fun seems to be the buzzword underlining the ceremonies, an endless carousel of dancing and drinking in the foreground.

When asked 'What motivates you to get married?', the replies were surprisingly conventional. Most were looking for stability, happiness, financial security, a sex partner etc. Ratna Chadha had a different take. Focusing on the young generation from the upper class living in metro cities, she says, 'Most youngsters have education, are travelling all the time, they have the independence, the girls know that they have inheritances, they have already slept with each other, marriage is just a legal stamp for them. Maybe to get kids, but even there they know one can freeze eggs and all that. And a big wedding is like an understanding between a mother and daughter ... just like a father gives a business to his son, the mother plans the big wedding for her daughter.' This line of thinking was challenged by her daughter Aditi, who argued, 'The problem is why are parents not getting out of this way of thinking? Why this dream for a girl? Why not something to build her up rather than her wedding? This needs to change.'

Ankit, the wedding planner who is a young millennial himself, has a rather cynical take on this as he says, 'These rich kids, they do it because that's the next thing to do. After completing their education, they have joined the business, and then comes the poser, what next? "Ok so let's marry." They have no clue about love, they think being physical is love. Their idea of life is to travel to fancy locations, wear designer clothes, have a good car and wear massive diamonds.' I ask, 'And same-sex love, what is the view on that?' Ankit laughs and says, 'My mother actually asks me what does it mean, what can the couple do? For us Punjabis appearances are very important, it's like the movie, *Zindagi Na Milegi Dobara*. Like when I travel abroad, mom tells me to put up nice pics on Facebook, not the terribly tanned ones. So appearance are all important, same-sex love is not to be flashed to the public.'

A hurriedly engaged couple having second thoughts might feel trapped by the big wedding preparations. With such a frenzied buildup and family expectations contributing relentlessly to the mounting pressure, do couples have space to think and rethink such a critical decision? Can they change their mind and say no, opt for the individuated choice rather than pleasing the family? The answer perhaps lies in this apocryphal story. When Lady Diana Spencer began to harbour misgivings during the engagement period with Prince Charles and wanted to call off the wedding, her sister is supposed to have famously said, 'It's too late darling, your face is on the tea towels.'[22]

The tea towel today is the social media, a two-way picture guzzler of a platform, which relays the small, intimate, fun moments of the courtship, the engagement, the shopping, the dance practice and everything leading up to the mega wedding to the mobiles of friends, their friends, and friends of those friends, on a wave of hundreds of likes and loves.

4

BOLLYWOOD MASALA!

A woman's palm with a motif of fresh mehendi in progress fills the screen before the camera zooms out to a typical 'shaadi ka ghar', this time an ultra-Punjabi one, complete with glasses of lassi, tent-wallahs, laddoos being made, fairy lights being tested and bhangra beats of 'Poora London Thumakda', including the uncle swaying with the mandatory *sir pe gilasssi*, or glass balanced on his head. The sheer exuberance of the song with its electric tempo, grandmothers and little kids dancing with unadulterated joy, replete with a moment of power outage, is Bollywood's tribute to real Indian weddings. Sure enough, it has been playing at north Indian weddings for years now. Which only reinforces this deeply symbiotic relationship, where inspiration and influence, movies and real life interchange.

This is Bollywood – reviled, lampooned, spoofed but also revered and emulated by billions of people around the world – the immensely popular face of Indian cinema.[1,2] Though one cannot negate the immense contribution of regional cinemas from across the various film hubs of the country. It is a projection on the wide screen of the heartbeat of a people, their dreams and hopes and fears, suitably moulded and often liberally airbrushed for popular consumption, that captures the popular imagination with few parallels, except perhaps cricket, which provokes in some measure the same hysterical reactions and mass following.

What Inspires Bollywood?

The popularity of Bollywood, and indeed Indian cinema, can be traced to the national love for drama, with its inspiration coming from the great fount of the creative arts, the Natya Shastra, and its many explanations of what makes for a truly great performance.[3] It emphasizes the confluence of *bhava* (emotion) and *rasa* (essence). *Rasa* is the ultimate emotional experience that an artiste provokes with her work. The effect is like getting liberated from earthly bonds, as the audience, moved by the music and the movements (*murchhanas*) of the dance forms, is aroused into experiencing, at least for a short while, and becoming one with the highest expression of the human spirit, in the most profound way.

Films have enthusiastically embraced the moods as invoked by the *rasas*, making it possible for the audience to experience an exhilarating mix of emotions through performance and art. This magic formula, evolved and honed by the early dream merchants, continues to mesmerize even contemporary audiences, however spoilt for choice they may be with their access to global cinema and the proliferation of television and digital channels of entertainment. The invitation to a popcorn world flavoured with the bittersweet chocolate of happiness and the downsides of life, seems to have hit upon some primal core of the human heart, essaying its dreams and aspirations while amplifying their unspoken emotions and often shaping them.

Bollywood has also become the vehicle of India's soft power, with huge audiences across the globe, especially the Indian diaspora, driven by nostalgic yearnings and an strong cultural connect. Indian visitors to the former Soviet Union are often surprised when they hear the familiar ditty 'Mera Joota Hai Japani' on foreign lips welcoming them to their land. I experienced the same to my great delight, when a fruit-seller in Uzbekistan presented his sweetest oranges to me while he sang a lovely Russian accented version.

Out of the nine *rasas* described in the ancient texts, the makers of Hindi and other language films have been particularly partial to centering their films around the shringar *rasa* – the impulse invoking the most complex human emotions – the headiness of love and the bleakness of separation or *viraha*. Love's twisted journey and the anticipated happy ending are fodder for an audience which instantly relates to the emotions of the lead couple. Rachel Dwyer, an eminent film critic points out in an essay, 'The movie could be about religion, about nationalism or about family. In the end, it is all about love.'[4]

Yet, it is intriguing that the ground realities of the country are so much at variance with the central theme of the movies, whose story lines remain so focussed on love. This is rather peculiar, because in real life we have very few expressions of it being encouraged or allowed to fructify unless it is within the controlled environment of a sanctioned relationship. Many eminent sociologists, moved by this lack of engagement with love and romance in real life, have commented on India's sexual barrenness.[5] One possible explanation for this constant flirting with romantic love in the movies can perhaps be attributed to cinema being the release for an explosive situation, this repression of love and sex, where the cinemagoers feel themselves transmuted into the shoes of the cavorting stars on the screen, singing their joyous articulations of love, or sighing empathetically at their searing passion and the tears of parting.

The Changing Storyline

The trajectory of Indian cinema is a reflection of the social and cultural transitions actually taking place in the country – from social dramas and soppy love stories of the post-Independence period to present-day globalized narratives catering to a whole range of audiences – massy, classy, niche and multiplex. Globalization changed the romance on the big screen irretrievably, bringing in a very international idiom to its core. From the 1950s right until the 1970s, Bollywood portrayed a well-grooved pattern – the initial years when soulful star pairs like Nargis-Raj Kapoor or Dilip Kumar-Madhubala set the silver screen ablaze with their sizzling chemistry. Their looks, mannerisms, the storylines of their movies, the marvellously hummable and poetic songs, a world of syrupy romance was punctuated with tragic men and self-sacrificing women, whose destinies were forever impacted by the heavy hand of fate. These were the stars, who seemed to bring the firmament down to earthly plains with that unforgettable fusion of romance and tragedy spiced with dollops of charisma. A generation of young women and men turned star-worshippers, genuflected to their deities like Rajesh Khanna, Sharmila Tagore and Hema Malini among others, sending them messages written in blood.

But as the country was buffeted by political upheavals, romance gave way to scorching tales of revenge and rage, personified by the fire-spitting anti-hero Amitabh Bachchan. Romance was pushed to the side lines, the heroine was reduced to a mere prop, and the box office was straddled by this colossal figure who spoke to the common man, who portrayed the lives of those at the bottom of the pile, the majority of the audience. However, this formulaic script came under fire when the economy opened up in the early 1990s and the profile of the audience changed. It was time for the revival of the middle-classes, who once again asserted their presence at the box office. As a film critic says in her study of the film industry, 'The Hindi film industry's metamorphosis into Bollywood would not have been possible without the rise of neo-liberal economic ideals in India.'[6] This economic revolution also ushered a new unfamiliar world for the emerging middle-classes. They wanted to experiment and experience different flavours of life but were uncomfortable in the rapidly shifting social structures and the changing economy, which was threatening their traditional life patterns. Job opportunities in larger cities meant going away from the comfortable milieu of provincial towns. So where could they find refuge but in the familiar arms of the family. This was the rock-solid institution that provided order, solidity and anchoring to a new and emerging middle-class. As Patricia Uberoi, a sociologist says, 'For most, the family remains and not merely by default, the sole institution that signifies the unity, uniqueness and moral superiority of Indian culture in a time of change, uncertainty and crisis.'[7] Sensing this mood and the disenchantment with formulaic cinema, producers and young directors tried a create films that catered to the middle-class value system. Dwyer elaborates, 'By the end of 1990s mainstream cinema returned to romance and music, with new young stars, fresh marketing strategies. A new style of cinema celebrated a consumerist, transnational society, where love, romance, fashion and fun were the goals of the young wealthy Indians, who, even if resident outside India, demonstrated to their parents Indian family values.'

As the economy changed, bureaucratic controls loosened and the State came out to support the movie industry, thereby rescuing it financially from the grip of Dubai-based 'bhais'.[8] But the government could not quite align itself with the '*dhishoom dhishoom*' drama, from which the middle-class had distanced itself. It was time for the entry of a new set of movies that were family-oriented and reflective of the cherished 'Indian values'. Ones that would appeal to the artistic sensibilities of a sophisticated and urbane audience. The mushrooming of plush multiplexes made the demand even more urgent. The money and marketing skills had been requisitioned, but how were they to fill the yawning abyss left by the demise of the 'revenge story'?

And Bollywood is Born

The crisis was ably met by the creative heads of the Bombay filmdom, with ingenuity and a breadth of imagination that signalled a remarkable change of the narrative. Love and romance – the perennial favourites of the Indian audience – were reclaimed, set in – new and exotic locales that held a great appeal for the middle-class audience. To all of this was added a generous dose of songs and dances. And thus, Bollywood was born. The purists snickered and the old timers of the movie industries rubbished the awful moniker, but the drivers of the industry and the audience loved it. They wanted 'Bollywood' with the trappings of 'angrezi' movies: slick production and contemporary styling, which recognized their well-travelled, well-heeled sensibility.

Love Shows the Way

Qyamat se Qayamat Tak released in 1988, and it was the first of this genre of treacly romances, followed by *Maine Pyaar Kiya*, directed by

Sooraj Barjatya in 1989, that became a sensation and a trendsetter of sorts. It was a signal to filmmakers to explore the possibilities of working with gentler scripts that gave primacy to the play of emotions and tender expressions. Love had shown the way, and now, the next step would be to conjugate it with the wedding, an image that so dominated the Indian view of love. Filmmakers were now exploring ways to give the movie-goer a virtual experience of an Indian wedding, through the kaleidoscope of colour, drama and opulence. Barjatya topped the remarkable success of *Maine Pyar Kiya*, with his bigger, grander and even more successful *Hum Aapke Hain Kaun* (HAHK) released in 1994. With a runtime of nearly 3.5 hours, centered around a large family that readily breaks into song and dance, chronicling the sub-themes of Indian values through the prism of love and the cherished family dream – the wedding – the film was a blockbuster. The audience lapped it up, sending cash registers ringing across the country. One year later, came another runaway hit, *Dilwale Dulhaniya Le Jayenge* (DDLJ), from debut director Aditya Chopra, drenched in romance and youthful rebellion, with a wedding once again at the centre of its narrative. The success of these two films ushered a huge change in the film industry – their metaphors for love, romance and weddings percolated into the larger wedding narrative across the country and forever changed our wedding celebrations. This was true most definitely in north and central India, but it rippled farther than their makers would have imagined.

Other than HAHK and DDLJ, I have looked at three other movies which have so interestingly dovetailed romance and marriage, and in the bargain influenced the wedding industry in infinitesimal ways that we are still trying to unravel. These movies, with the exception of *Antardwanda* (inner conflict), have built their narrative around the tensions of young love, with the wedding positioned as the dénouement, while also touching upon a variety of social and cultural issues that reflect the anxieties, hopes and value systems of the spaces they occupy. The Indian family, with its cross-generational and affinal relationships is a constant, against which the turbulent passion of young love is played out. The inter-generational conflict, an inevitable part of this face-off and akin to real life, is where romance and youthful aspirations are involved in a tug of war. We see this scenario depicted in HAHK, DDLJ and to a certain degree in *Hum Dil De Chuke Sanam*. In the latter, the conflict is between traditional, family-approved love and the carefree, organic attraction between bodies, minds and souls, love too untamed to find societal approval. These films operate within a moral universe where romance triumphs and justice is done, at least by the final scene. The audience has its emotions anchored in the young lovers, living their despair and tribulations, and fervently hoping that love will conquer all.

Films Break the Box office

HAHK was the first Hindi film to cross the billion-rupee barrier, grossing more than ₹3,600 crores worldwide.[9] What fashioned its phenomenal success is a question that has puzzled industry trade analysts, rival filmmakers, critics and academics, as they tried to analyze its indefinable alchemy that led to it becoming the gold standard in box office collections. Patricia Uberoi adopted an unconventional if effective approach to get the pulse of the audience. She writes about how she stood outside the movie hall as the audience streamed out, asking them a set of questions, the primary one being, 'Why do you like this movie so much?' The movie-goers overwhelmingly voted for what in their view reflected the very essence of their Indianness and Indian values

– the family and the harmonious way they lived together in the large joint family.[10] The viewers also approved of the romance between the hero and the heroine, based on a non-sexualized model, where the couple make no attempt to kiss or make physical overtures.

Shorn of the tugs and pulls of the often-dysfunctional families that are the reality, HAHK was an invitation to join an idyllic family that is nearly utopian. This movie became a benchmark in fashioning the concept of the ideal wedding. In its employment of rituals, the teasing humour between the bride's and the groom's families, the *khatirdari*, the film found an immediate resonance with the aspirational viewer. The depiction seemed so overwhelmingly real that many said that the film made them feel that they were watching a video of their own wedding ceremony. The immense popularity of the film had an unintended effect, which in many ways reiterated the power of cinema and its role in engendering new cultural norms. HAHK set off a tsunami of wedding and fashion trends, which eclipsed in its blazing popularity, every other film-related trend that had been grist for youthful fancies.

The 1960s had seen women changing hairstyles to adopt the famous 'Sadhana' cut, a kind of forehead fringe that every neighborhood hairdresser learnt to style; in the 1970's Rajesh Khanna the superhero sent a wave of men copying his haircut and the baggy guru kurta, invented to accommodate spreading middles! Bobby – young Dimple Kapadia's name in the eponymous film – was what scores of new parents named their little girls. And finally, when Amitabh Bachchan strode on to the scene, his angry young man look, styled with bell-bottoms and dog-coloured shirts, was copied by thousands of young men. But none of these influenced the fundamental avatar of India's most beloved celebration – the wedding, or altered the style and scale of its fashions, its rituals and its budget, the way HAHK did. Perhaps its release at a time that was juxtaposed with a booming economy, ushered it into a global era of slick marketing that became a game-changer of sorts.

By contrast, the earlier movies were hamstrung by the limitations of the mainstream media, which could provide little behind-the-scenes access to the film-obsessed public, beyond the state-owned radio channel *Vividh Bharti* and sundry film magazines like *Filmfare*, *Stardust* and *Screen*. Television was still a nascent medium and film companies were dependent on amateurish marketing strategies and poor distribution. In the 1990s though, the movie-goers' deeper pockets also spurred the box office earnings of such films. Madhuri Dixit's famous green lehenga in the song 'Joote Lo Paise Do' in HAHK gained cult status as the outfit to be copied for every wedding in north India, while Salman Khan's white suit was the groom's sartorial aspiration. Rituals that were once culture- and region-specific – the viewing of the potential bride and groom, the stealing of the groom's shoe, the *vidaai* – went beyond their geographical and cultural specifics and were copied at weddings across the country. The movie even juggled the order of the wedding functions and their importance in the celebration scale. The song 'Didi Tera Devar Deevana,' played in the typical setting of what was called the 'Ladies Sangeet' – a small family affair, but the movie gave it cult status and unexpectedly fuelled a trend for having such a function. In the process the sangeet skyrocketed in style and spending to take the second most important place in the wedding pantheon.

Sacrificing for Family's Sake

The makers of HAHK also added a traditional Indian trope which unfailingly appeals to the Indian audience – the young couple willing to sacrifice their love for the sake of family. Nisha (played by Madhuri Dixit) learns that she is to be married to her brother-in-law, a convenient ploy to transpose her into her dead sister's shoes so that she can take care of her baby. She is obviously appalled at the idea, as she is in love with Prem (Salman Khan), but suppresses her desires for the sake of the family. Prem is quiet for similar reasons, and seems to have resigned himself to the prospect of his sweetheart becoming his brother's wife. The primacy of the family and its greater happiness demands that they sacrifice their relationship.

The ideal of sacrifice is the masala that has spiced Indian stories from the very beginning and finds its place even in the great epics. It played out in *nautankis* or folk theatre too, which have laid the groundwork for many a film. This sacrifice of the individual for the greater good of the family runs like a faultline through many great stories of India, establishing an instant connect with the audience. In the Ramayana, Rama leaves Sita, which though based on false rumours and idle gossip, was purportedly for the greater good of his kingdom. Sita herself sacrifices the luxuries of the palace to brave the rigours of exile and later brings up her twins as a single mother. The Mahabharata has a plethora of such stories with the central homily – sacrifice for the family keeps it united. Kunti unknowingly commands Arjuna to share Draupadi, who he has won as his wife in a swayamvar, with his four brothers. And every word uttered by their mother is a binding command that the sons must obey. Yudhishthira stakes his brothers in a game of dice and after losing, hands them over to the enemy, a condition that his brothers accept – their sacrifice to honour their brother's word. Fortunately for the audience, in HAHK the young lovers are united in the end, allowing movie-goers to shuffle out of the theatre with the satisfied feeling of seeing a beautifully wrought drama with a happy ending.

Wanted: An Arranged Love Marriage

This celebration of the ideal joint family places family's pride and prestige over individual choice. Therefore, arranged marriage is the preferred path, where the superior wisdom of the parents and elders must dictate love's course. Family over self is a part of the societal pact that Indians have been taught to accept, making 'adjust' and 'compromise' two favourite words in the family vocabulary. This is a fact corroborated by many sociological studies. Hence when Prem, the hero in HAHK whose name literally means love, is asked what kind of marriage he would like, he answers bashfully, though he is madly in love with Nisha, 'an arranged love marriage!' A strange moniker for audiences unused to Indian sensibilities perhaps, but one perfectly understandable to the audience who loved and cried with the young lovers and nodded in approval as they sought the blessings of their parents and elders.

In *Hum Dil De Chuke Sanam*, the passionate love between the protagonists Sameer (played by Salman Khan) and Nandini (Aishwarya Rai) does not win the approbation of her parents. Sameer is a foreigner of unknown provenance, and Nandini, in falling for him, is seen as breaking the ironclad bonds of familial fidelity. Set against the lush colours of a Gujarati haveli and beautiful foreign locales, Sanjay Leela Bhansali, the director, presents a searing portrayal of thwarted love, a forced arranged marriage and its heartbreaking consequences.

Many young couples, when questioned about how they had found their eventual partners, considering 75 per cent marriages continue to be arranged,[11] declare unselfconsciously and without a trace of irony, 'Ours is an arranged love marriage'. What does this phrase really mean, and how does love enter this sanitized arrangement? This is a question that has no easy answers, couched as it is in the interstices of tradition, culture, caste, status, feelings and a host of other intangibles. In practical terms, it often translates into the family-approved couple being allowed to interact over the phone, or in more progressive families, in person, for a stipulated length of time after being introduced. Often they are chaperoned by a sister, sister-in-law or some other equally amenable young relative, but whose presence is no obstacle to the raging emotions in young hearts. This is a scenario where the frisson of sly physical contact translates itself into that first expression of sexual desire, this time summarily approved by the family. Who can nitpick and say this is not love?

The symbiotic relationship between Indian weddings and Hindi films found vigorous articulation in *DDLJ*, which remains one of the longest-running Indian movies, still drawing packed audiences in the cinema hall where it was first released, nearly a quarter of a century ago.[12] Love is an integral part of the narrative, introduced in one of first scenes by a prancing young heroine (played by Kajol) singing about an imagined lover, 'Mere khwaabon mein jo aaye, aake mujhe chhed jaaye', as her bemused mother looks on. The tensions between romance, free choice and familial obligations, played out against the background of an impending arranged wedding, has held the audience in thrall across generational barriers. Once again, we see the conflict between young love and the family's wishes. In a nod to real-life parents who believe in arranging matches for their children, the father in DDLJ too has blinkered views about what love and marriage are about. He is a stubborn patriarchal character, hellbent on keeping his decades-old promise of marrying off his daughter to his best friend's son. In this case his control over the family is couched in the assertion of his morally superior Indian values which shore the family against the decadent West, living as they are in London. And the prospective groom is thousands of miles away in India. The reassertion of the 'desh ki mitti', the longing for home for the NRIs who really haven't left their Indian hearts behind, is seamlessly woven into the narrative.

The immigration to foreign shores is a part of the desire for upward mobility that was a legacy of Indians migrating en masse to England/US in the fifties and sixties, and yet the purity of their Indian middle-class values remained unsullied. So in a sense, though the son leaves the motherland for better prospects, he is not guilty of betraying or abandoning her or her values. This belief, deeply embedded in the Indian mind, finds expression even in the historical narratives of Mahatma Gandhi, who too, when leaving for foreign shores had promised his mother that he would not betray his essential 'Indian' morality. Translated it meant that he was not to succumb to a 'Western' lifestyle and its host of enticing prospects such as drinking alcohol, eating meat, or dalliances with the opposite sex.

The movies discussed so far are truly last century, when a prevailing innocence and naiveté made the garish costumes and the syrupy sweetness of HAHK palatable enough for it to create box office records, while DDLJ had women swooning over the hero who leapt across balconies to break the Karwa Chauth fast with his beloved, an unusual occurrence in those patriarchal lands.

Since the DDLJ days, India and Bollywood have both had a huge makeover. Points of view have transformed, experimental and bold subjects that were forbidden in the past entered the main-stream, and talking about sex became less of a taboo. This in many ways freed sex from the binaries – the evil serpent leading young women and men astray with its invidious temptations of the flesh. For the women in Hindi cinema of the 1970s there was no greater danger than that single sexual encounter, which invariably left her pregnant, the man vanishing next morning, and the society going *tch tch* condemning her for her moral turpitude. *Julie*, *Aradhana* and *Andaz* – all released in the 1970s were steeped in these depressing results of a woman going to bed with a man without the mandatory sindoor in her hair. A loss of paradise for the heroine without even the modicum of that fig leaf to shield her from the baleful eyes of the righteous.

The metamorphosis of India into a country in sync with global trends, with a young population raring to go, was inevitably reflected in its movies, with directors anchoring their plotlines on a population high on adrenalin, experimental in nature and yet starved of the opportunities that would provide them an outlet for their fantasies. Unlike in the movies of the past, where conscience-racked characters were compelled to choose between love and family, the plots no longer seemed loaded with that onerous burden of guilt.

As the columnist Santosh Desai wrote, 'When Aditya falls in love with Geet in *Jab We Met*, a boy falls in love with a girl. For a Hindi film that is an uncommon thing to happen. Usually, when a hero and heroine fall in love, they carry with them the burden of something larger, either by way of a class divide, or the unpaid debts of an earlier birth, or perhaps the idea of modernity and tradition. The young being allowed to choose their mates is an idea India has had trouble accepting.'[13] This point is point richly illustrated in the examples given earlier. But in *Jab We Met*, Imtiaz

Ali, like the crop of young directors who are impatient with the tales of moral burden, turned the lens to individual choice as the primary motive for boy to meet girl. This was in sync with new urban realities, where young people had several avenues to form friendships and fall in love. This new romance of consent between adult women and men that didn't have to be hidden retained its appeal for a desi audience. Of course, the elements of family presence was marvellously in sync with the young couple in love. So even as Geet elopes in the dead of the night and goes traipsing off to Manali to chase an uninterested boyfriend, eventually she falls for Aditya. And even though he was thoroughly assessed and accepted by her family, their love was truly unburdened by social pressures.

Enter the Game Changer

In December 2010 came the movie *Band Bajaa Baaraat* (BBB), with a young star cast of Ranveer Singh as Bittoo Sharma and Anushka Sharma as Shruti Kakkar, who whole-heartedly belong to a Delhi that is encased in a roti-shotti, halwa-puri, *Mudrika*-metro earthy middle-class culture, far removed from the leafy boulevards and Gymkhana memberships of Lutyens' Delhi. The young couple meet, and far from turning into gooey-eyed lovers at first sight, start a wedding-planning business together. As their business flourishes, not without its disappointments and stresses, love wafts in. But how does love weave through the realities of ambition and competitiveness? The film reflected the complex realities of the young generation, who flocked to theatres to make it a huge hit. BBB has a wonderfully modern feel to it, depicting a very equitable relationship, a rarity in Bollywood. The film is an ode to an India where wedding budgets are increasing exponentially. And so arrive the creative duo, Bittoo and Shruti, who can make any wedding better and grander, irrespective of the budget. BBB was the first movie in a really long time to have insightfully captured the changing wedding scenario in India, altered as it had been by economics and the aspirations of the nouveau riche desperately trying to outshine the Mathurs and the Khannas in their social circle. It had a fresh story arc in a familiar, relatable setting. Their life problems were distinctively personal too, which Bittoo and Shruti try to solve like young working couples do, amidst the strife and stress of working lives in the metros.

Ankit Malhotra, CEO of the Delhi-based wedding planning company Comme Sogno Vero, says, 'After BBB, weddings were just not the same anymore. The ambitious scale of the wedding that we see today is because of BBB. Even wedding planners happened only after people saw Ranveer and Anushka give it the professional touch. People only change their minds when they see others doing it. Big budget, big show, it all adds up.'

Bollywood and its glitzy depiction of the Indian wedding changed something fundamental in how many Indians viewed weddings, prodding others to live out the fantasy of the big celebration. But not everyone was changed by this expanding vision. Certain parts of the country are still stuck within stifling mind traps of the most regressive practices that continue till date.

This was the focus of the film *Antardwanda*. It was released in 2010 and went on to win the National Award for Best Film on Social Issues. It was based on a true-life incident of a man being kidnapped and forced to marry a woman, whom he neither knew nor had any knowledge of her existence.[14] Set against the feudal backdrop of Bihar, the movie shows how grooms were kidnapped and forced into marrying unknown women, so the girl's family could avoid dowry, which had so bedevilled the society in these feudal lands.[15] The movie broadly follows this theme while foregrounding it against the changing social dynamics where young women and men learn to carve their own lives in the anonymous, non-judgemental landscapes of the big metros. And so our young man, from the boondocks of provincial India with the lingering smells of '*asli* Bharat' still clinging to him, comes to Delhi with dreams of making it to the civil services. Amidst this ambitious plan, he falls in love, and when he discovers that his girlfriend is pregnant, rushes home with the noble intention of informing his parents about his decision to marry her. The stage is set for urban and rural India to collide as this scene is juxtaposed with the bathetic enacting of the social hierarchies where the potential bride's family now back in rural settings – way down on the social ladder – attempts to entice the groom's family with dowry, many promises and insufferable obsequiousness. The scene depicts the father of the bride hunched at the feet of the groom's father, from where he keeps upping the dowry, while the boy's father, bristling with matchless arrogance and greed, is contemptuously dismissive. What follows is a script of Machiavellian villainy that seems implausible even though it is plucked from life.

The unfolding script is a bitter comment on the various pillars of this system, where the compulsions of social customs like marriage erode human values, the sanctity of relationships, and entraps the characters into the grey zones of an amoral universe, where traditional beliefs are turned on their head and become the other face of depravity. The wife, now manipulated into a situation where she must ensure the consummation of the marriage, makes the required advances, while her family and the hired goons watch with chilling intrusiveness for sex to happen, since this act alone can bestow legitimacy to the marriage. The consummation is finally a brutal assault, marital rape in all its unforgivable sordidness, which the wife forgives as her husband's right.

When I spoke to Swati Sen, the heroine of the movie, who won plaudits for her role as the repressed daughter and wife, she confided that she had taken more than twenty takes before she could infuse a careless acceptance into her voice as she mouthed the dialogue, '*Aap to husband hain mere, aapka right hai*'. 'You are my husband, you have the right [to force sex].' She had found it nearly impossible to digest the character's placid acceptance of the assault. The redeeming feature was the final act of defiance by the woman played by Swati Sen, who walks her own path, and this feature perhaps helped the movie win the National award.

And later came movies like *Queen* or *Tanu Weds Manu*. While they still focussed on marriage, they also challenged the stereotypes, with a rebellious heroine at its centre who refused to bow down to social pressures. Kangana Ranaut won much acclaim for ably playing the lead in both these films.

Music, the Food of Love

While movies and Indian weddings are intricately connected, the bonding truly comes into its own with film songs, which are used at various functions in a wedding celebration. Bollywood has a song for every occasion – from the first sight to first meeting, from the blossoming pyaar to an exuberant baraat arriving with a costumed band of musicians playing classics like 'Mere yaar ki shaadi hai' or 'Mere desh ki dharti'. Conversely, Bollywood would be equally bereft without the tradition of folk songs that are intrinsic to weddings. In a social milieu which otherwise allots fairly strict roles to each relationship, certain relationships are stamped with an interesting innuendo – such as that of the *devar*-

bhabhi or *jija-saali*, which allow for a liberal dose of risqué flavour to spice them up.

HAHK captures myriad moods and relationships beautifully in its songs. The shoe-stealing sequence and the song '*Joote do paise lo*' shows the sexual tension between the hero and the heroine Prem and Nisha, where under the garb of teasing and banter, their mutual attraction is fanned and expressed. In 'Mai ri mai', the girl's gentle entreaties to her mother as she is ready to embrace an adult love forms the undercurrent of the family's relationship with its daughter, where the inevitability of her departure is welded to the joyfulness of the wedding celebrations. In the later movie BBB, the customary banter turns combative, with the hero and the heroine exchanging verbal missiles with equal panache – a complete departure from the swagger of Shahrukh and the demure coyness of Kajol in DDLJ. Listen to Bittu aka Ranveer Singh brag: *Ladkon ki ungli pe naache hai zamaana... Kudiyan hai jebon mein rakh le* (We make the girls dance to our tune, and do as we please with them). To which the heroine replies looking both provocative and ethereally sexy, a visual image that blunts his challenge: *Ladkon ko lagta hai easy jeet jaana, Iss baar unko hara ke hai dikhaana* (The boys are deluded that they can win easily, this time round they have met their match).

Given the close family ties which define north Indian families, the *vidaai* is tinged with sadness, a dichotomous emotional schism that also celebrates her new status as a wife and the love that she has found with her husband. In earlier generations, the image of her leaving her parental home for her future *sasuraal*, or in-laws', was imbued with a sense of dread, a Damocles' sword poised over her fate. This song from the 1950s from the movie *Babul*, is typical of that time, where a sense of foreboding, compulsion and dread fills the heroine's words as she departs for her in-laws' – '*Chhodh babul ka ghar, mohe pi ke nagar aaj jana pada'* (I have been compelled to leave my natal home, to go to my husband's home).

Over the years, the songs of *vidaai* have changed, linked as they are to new social realities. The pathos of yesteryears has been transmuted into a more joyful acknowledgement that the lovers are now united. The bride now confides in her mother about her newfound love. Gone is the bashfulness or the sense of dread, which reflected an age where the woman had no agency. Young hopefuls for marriage in the country are saying in no uncertain terms that they want none of those pathos-riddled songs of yore. I quote these lines from a question posted by a bride-to-be on a social media site: 'Can someone please tell me of a good hindi bidaai/*vidaai* song? I want a nice song for my wedding video. I would prefer for it to be recent, but old ones are welcome too. I don't want the song: *babul de do vida*, (Oh! Father bid goodbye to your daughter) so please don't suggest that.'

In response to this question songwriters are suggesting a new emboldened bride in their lyrics. In *Baar Baar Dekho*, a 2016 science-fiction romance film, Katrina Kaif is dancing at her sangeet, singing unabashedly, '*Munde plenty mere liye ho gaye senti, tere liye main set hun is baat ki guarantee*' (Plenty of guys are in love with me, but I guarantee you I'm perfect only for you).

Songs tie so many wedding function together, infusing them with rhythm and verve, with apt lyrics that capture prevailing sentiments and get the party going. An irredeemable debt that we owe to the film industry.

And so it continues, the relationship between movies and weddings as a symbiotic bond, where they fuse and evolve to forge unchartered paths of the creative and the inspirational. The arc of emotions so inherent to the wedding, finds its perfect expressions in Bollywood songs. While Bollywood, despite the thematic range it is currently venturing into, continues to find its universal appeal in love and romance and its ultimate expression – the wedding. And Indian cinema and Indian weddings have both been greatly enriched by this *jugalbandi*.

5

BREAKING LOVE'S BARRIERS

They were young and in love. Manoj and Babli wanted to marry despite the rigid dos and don'ts laid down by their elders in their hometown of Kaithal in Haryana. Marriage is acceptable within the same caste and religion, but never in the same *gotra*.[1] This message had been repeated ad nauseum from childhood, to protect them from societal wrath, but when love happened those childhood lectures lost all meaning. Belonging to the same *gotra* within the Jat community, Manoj and Babli's marriage was strictly prohibited by the village elders, the Khap Panchayat – an illegal, all-male community organization representing a clan or a group of clans, who often took law and enforcement in their own hands.[2,3,4,5]

In 2007, Manoj and Babli eloped, secretly got married and then informed their families. The first consequence of flouting the Khap rules was social boycott – villagers were prohibited from interacting with them. Then Babli's family threatened violent reprisals for bringing dishonour to the family. The court gave them protection, but it was a sham, as later events revealed since her relatives finally caught up with them and killed the two lovers with medieval brutality, as described by Manoj's sister in hair-raising detail in an episode of the popular television show *Satyamev Jayate*. The story didn't quite end there though. The Khap Panchayat supported Babli's family and ordered punitive action against Manoj's family. However, despite the numerous death threats, Manoj's widowed mother Chandravati and sister decided that they were not going to be intimidated, they would instead carry the battle to the courts. After a protracted trial, the court finally held Babli's family responsible for the twin murders and pronounced death sentences for the five accused. But later, the Punjab and Haryana High Court commuted the death sentence and even acquitted two of the accused.[6]

Forbidden Love

Just a few months later in Kolkata, a similar story played out, except this time it was religion and class that didn't allow a 'happily ever after'. Rizwanur Rahman, a Muslim teacher of modest means at a computer centre fell in love with his student Priyanka Todi, who was from a wealthy Marwari family. They decided to get married in defiance of all social conventions, failing to grasp the chasm of class and religion between them, and the power of the forces they had challenged. Their marriage was no protection against their fates. Rizwanur was warned to either leave the girl or else face dire consequences. Soon, the threats turned real and Rizwanur's mangled body was found stretched across the railway tracks. There were no witnesses.[7]

These are not isolated instances. Every year thousands of couples defy the strict social norms of whom to love, restricted by the parameters of caste, community, religion, *gotra* etc., literally putting their lives at risk. Murders related to love are the third-highest reason for peoples' deaths in the country.[8] The government has tried to address the violence and retribution that is normally provoked by such marriages, by evolving an ecosystem that provides protection homes, police guards and quick legal redressal, but a wide gap remains. The safeguards crumble before the cross-currents of sentiment and outrage that are deeply embedded within some people. The problem is not the law per se, but its protectors and implementers – the police and the other arms of the legal system, those bound by duty to protect the rights of an adult to choose one's partner, as guaranteed by the Constitution. But while the law may be even-handed, its forces are human, filled with people who echo similar prejudices as the rigid society they belong to. And so, police protection remains a poor form of defence, vanishing when most needed. As happened in the case of Babli and Manoj, who were supposedly protected by court orders but were really at the mercy of their avenging relatives. Babli's brother and other male relatives killed them, while the police connived with the 'honour killing'.

Nivedita Menon, the eminent feminist sociologist, gives us an insight into the social processes that drive this control: 'Khap Panchayats create an environment of fear and oppression in order to uphold local hegemony and create a culture of silence and resignation. Relationships between men and women are determined by what is considered "appropriate", which perpetuates patriarchal lineage and property.'[9]

Runaway weddings, as these are referred to by the media, are scripting a paradigm shift in behavioural patterns and attitudes amongst the young, breaking new grounds in the social history of this country. With rigid caste classifications and the observance of endogamous customs, marital alliances have been predetermined by the family or village elders for centuries. Individual choice was rarely considered, though history has a few rather romanticized versions of men defying the conventional rules and galloping into the horizon with their loved one. The stories of Shakuntala and Dushyant, of Prithviraj Chauhan taking away his beloved Sanyogita from her wedding altar, are part of our folklore.[10] Even Parvati, the goddess, defied her father's selection of the groom and instead devoted herself to winning over Shiva, her partner of choice. Yet, these stories are few and far between.

The last couple of decades or so have brought an unprecedented change in the marriage scenario, with many young couples turning established dictums on their head. Social scientists and analysts have been examining this fascinating phenomenon. Today the young are falling in love without a care for social norms or the conventions of centuries. While they seek their family's acceptance, some couples have to battle archaic mindsets unwilling to accept these unsanctioned unions. Faced with parental opposition, the tangles of caste and community, the State's failure to protect them, and the lack of a support structure, these couples think that the only way to be together is to elope.

In this love-repressed country the unfortunate corollary of young people's desires is resentment and often a violent backlash. The resulting volatile situation has traditionalists raging against rapidly changing attitudes of the youth. Bewildered and threatened by this change, they try to impose their morals, shrouded in patriarchy, misogyny, and a phobia of the West, upon those who don't follow their rules. So when a couple in the throes of love is kept apart by an unrelenting world, they have to make some hard choices to be together. The transformation of this young couple, whose lives are otherwise charted along a predictable path of controlled upbringing can be quite radical. For them choosing love and marriage on their own terms is not a fairy tale that ends with 'a happily ever after', but is instead riven with uncertainties, dogged by the fear of some tragedy, where friends and family turn into enemies, sometimes baying for their blood.[11]

Badri, my friend from Agra, recounts the story of his 28-year-old brother Kunal, who was working in Mumbai in a private company, when he fell in love with his colleague, a woman from a conservative Maharashtrian Brahmin family. In a year's time, they decided to get married, but her parents refused to accept the match. Amongst a host of objections, Kunal's community was one – he was a Sindhi from U.P. – his father a teacher, he was a college graduate, and he worked at a clerical level. His education and work matched with the girl Pari's, but her community and her father's government job gave her a 'superior edge'. And therein lay the crux. Marriage was often a way of getting a girl to marry 'up' into a higher social stratum, but her father saw her choice as a step down. He wouldn't even consider the marriage, and in order to control his daughter's wilfulness, threatened to make her quit her job and lock her up at home. Such punitive measures are not unusual, and however humiliating, young women have been subjected to this. A couple of weeks had elapsed since that house arrest, when Badri received a desperate call from Kunal. Pari and he were on a train to Agra. They were also being tailed by the police as her father had accused Kunal of abducting his daughter. Badri was now really worried, as he knew that with the police involved, his brother could be in deep trouble. He could be arrested or worse beaten up to within an inch of his life. Badri tells me how he went through the contacts on his mobile, trying to find sources within the police or the government who could help Kunal and Pari. The advice was simple enough: 'Get them married first and then ask for police protection'. Badri met the couple as they stepped off the train. They drove straight to a temple, where he had made the arrangements for their wedding, Kunal and Pari were married according to Hindu rites. Once the marriage was solemnised, they went to the nearest police station, where they declared themselves as married. Since Pari was of consenting age, and declared that she had not been abducted but had chosen to go with Kunal of her own free will, the police dropped the case. Though Pari's parents did not accept the match, their objections were overruled. Three years later, Kunal and Pari still remember their nightmarish train journey which makes their pulse race.

Organizing the Runaway Wedding

The secrecy and urgency involved in the rising number of runaway weddings has inadvertently developed a well-oiled mechanism in which marriage fixers – the lawyers, pandits or qazis – ensure that the wedding takes place with minimum fuss. A blogger has given an insightful description of the process in Sawantwadi, a small sleepy town near Goa, which has lately developed a reputation of being a safe haven for couples escaping parental wrath, to get married safely.[12] A marriage town, where locals reap rich financial rewards for facilitating love's legitimacy for desperate couples. No questions asked, with an entire system geared to beat the system – the bureaucratic needs, the licenses, the religious ceremony, the mandated photograph of the married couple, and even the wedding card printed in double quick time to provide the irrefutable proof of the wedding. This resourceful coterie even manages the bureaucratic processes of procuring the required affidavits and attestation from a gazetted officer, before sealing the match with a registration.

Couples on the Run

There are no official figures about how many couples actually elope to get married. But case studies, newspaper reports and court cases show that the runaway wedding is an addition to the different kinds of marriages taking place in the country. Looking at the numbers of cases disposed of over a given period, Meena Dhanda, writing for the *Economic and Political Weekly* found that if one were to consider an average of 105 cases per week in a Punjab court, there would be an estimated 5,250 cases per year of couples securing protection orders.[13] Another sociologist writes that, 'According to the Chandigarh lawyers, the Punjab and Haryana High Court receives as many as 50 applications per day from couples seeking protection. This is a staggering tenfold rise from about five to six applications a day, five years ago.'[14] Intriguingly, given its image of toxic masculinity and its terribly skewed sex ratio,[15] Punjab and Haryana have some of the largest number of runaway couples in the country behind only Goa and Meghalaya, two of India's very liberal states, in the number of couples who have defied the system and opted for their own partners. The figures quoted here have been further corroborated by quantitative data on inter-caste marriages which was based on the National Family Health Survey, NFHS III – 2005-06. And yet, these incidents denote an aberration in a country where no more than 5.4 per cent married women between ages 15–49, said 'yes', when asked if theirs was an inter-caste marriage, a figure that remain unchanged in the last forty years, as per the IHDS (India Human Development Survey 2005-5 and 2011-12 (IHDSI and II) which covered a representative sample of 41,554 households spread across 33 states. A striking 73 per cent of women say that parents (or other relatives) chose their husbands and almost 70 per cent of them met their husbands only on the day of their wedding/*gauna* (the ceremony when the bride departs for her in-laws').

What does emerge though, despite our strictly controlled social mores is that there seems to be a correlation between orthodoxy and rebellion – the regressive views, the suppression of women in a gender-skewed society and the extremely limited opportunities available for women and men to mingle in an open healthy environment, which, when not being pushed under the surface as stiflingly clandestine expressions of love, expresses itself as 'forbidden love', or love on the run.

Barriers to Love

The runaway couples, have captured the narrative of love stories, with their dramatic headlines, the spectre of revenge and skirmishes with the law. But there are other loves in other spaces, with their own brand of drama. There are young people trying to convince their families about their partner's religion, caste, community, class, skin colour, food choices, language, education, social standing, political leanings, desire to work, desire to not have children, desire to live in another country, refusal to exchange dowry et al. The list goes on. Sometimes a rational, reasonable conversation does the trick, but there is a whole range of negotiation tactics and emotions employed. Pleas, screaming matches, sentimental letters, walkouts, starvation, the silent treatment, tears, and in extreme cases, suicide threats. Not an unusual threat, as many young lovers have tried to inflict harm on themselves when up against the wall of parental opposition. Parental control remains a powerful tool to regulate the love-infused world of their young. Their motives could be rooted in age-old prejudices or prompted by the challenges of a rapidly changing environment, but in India it is considered perfectly acceptable for parents to make or break a relationship for their child. But beyond the family and relatives, how do the other pillars of society, namely the legal system work to support the couple in love? And in such a milieu, what happens to same-sex love or love that contravenes the religious order?

The law of course sees love between consenting adults as an individual choice, where none of the societal barriers of caste or religions can stand in the way. So there is the Special Marriage Act, for those opting for an inter-religious marriage. Though in keeping with the delicate ground the State has ventured into, it has instituted several provisions to make sure that all objections to the match are addressed, including announcements made in the papers, just in case. All of these measures do make it a long-drawn process filled with bureaucratic tedium, but given the volatile passions involved, the State can only play a cautious Cupid.

A look at the guidelines given by Punjab and Haryana High Courts (dated 15 October 2010) to both the states of Punjab and Haryana and Union Territory (UT) of Chandigarh shows their support for individual choice. It has made 'absolute' an eloping couple's right to approach the courts, in cases where their kin is hounding them. The police too has been given instructions to deal sternly with parents/relatives/other members of the society who threaten such couples, and provide whatever possible support by way of mediation and counselling. But how is the law translated where it is most required, is the question that we need to examine here. The police, one arm of the legal system, as seen in the earlier examples, has revealed itself to be a recalcitrant partner that works on its own biased whims. But how about the lawyers or the courts – those at the forefront, battling to get justice for the couples – how do they view the couples who have taken this huge step?

According to Perveez Mody, in her ethnography of love marriages at the Tis Hazari courts in Delhi, the couples themselves are supremely sensitive to the largely negative vibes coming their way from lawyers and court functionaries, who think that the couples have got together to just have sex and they are doing the wrong thing by going against their parents. Sometimes the functionaries say this out loud, at other times they are dismissive or contemptuous. In order to counter this bias, the couple often adopts a supremely philosophical front, where they project their union as divinely ordained, a spiritual order, where the flesh and bodily needs are removed as reasons for their attraction. Meena Dhanda too tells us about the attitudes of some of the lawyers towards their fugitive clients. Giving instances from the Ladies Bar Room of the High Court in Punjab, she provides a window to the caste prejudices that corrode the minds of even senior lawyers, who see not love as the driver, but a strong physical attraction or lust as it is more disparagingly called, between these couples on the run.[16] While Dhanda is herself an advocate of Ambedkar's theory propounded in his book, *The Annihilation of Caste*, of the mixing of blood as absolutely necessary to changing the beliefs of caste superiority, she is taken aback by the attitudes of lawyers who disapprove of love between upper castes and Dalits.

Judges too have their prejudices and that is obvious when they are working on such cases. Their judgments sometimes take the flavour of moral science lessons as they lecture the couple on the responsibility towards one's parents and the need to have their blessings for one's marriage. In 2015, while granting police protection to young couples on the run, Justice Rameshwar Singh Malik (in the court of Haryana and Punjab) said in unambiguous terms that the 'the freedom of the individual is subject to social norms'.[17] While no one can dispute this statement, the context in which it was delivered sounds like a rap on the knuckles. That they opted for their own partners and thereby exercised individual choice is seen as violating the 'established and time-tested social norms of a civilized society ... and this choice should be exerted only subject to the social control and moral values which are centuries old and have not lost their shine even today,' pronounced the learned judge.

The disapproval by State actors becomes even more rabid and vocal when a girl is seen to violate the established boundaries of caste and class. Social scientists write scathingly about this attitude, where political power and the patriarchal family find common ground in controlling females, through which they uphold the caste and kinship ideology.[18] This is central to their idea of marital alliances, though fortunately the legal system does not support their prejudices.

In such a climate, the right of individuals is of course the first to be tossed aside. This ideology was most recently played out in full public glare in the case of 23-year-old Sakshi Mishra, the daughter of the MLA Pappu Bhartaul, whose example was discussed in the preface of this book. Sakshi's clever use of technology to counter her father's threats, with social media updates asking him to lay off, was promptly followed by two other couples from U.P. who came out to say that they were being harassed by their kin.[19]

Change is being ushered, but the backlash, the resistance, the sullying of unsanctioned love constantly reinvents itself and pops up from different quarters. We have a strident moral force protesting inter-religious couples in what is provocatively called 'Love Jihad'. We have this same moral force in action when their foggy lens of 'Indian culture' is challenged – couples punished for being together in parks, shamed when found in hotel rooms, girls pushed out of pubs, diktats against Western wear etc. are grist for these vigilante groups. And ever so often, the spectre of the evil West taking over our innocent Indianness is rattled like a broken record. The movie *Masaan* captures this stifling play of the State as moral arbiter within the confines of a society robbed of choice and sexual freedom, with the police raiding a hotel to book young unmarried couples caught 'sinning'. The subsequent decline into a dystopian world of blackmail and extortion makes for a chilling picture of how reality can similarly unfold. Which it sometimes does, as in the case where police raided a hotel in Pune and caught young unmarried couples who were having a 'good' time, for which offence their pictures were splashed in the national media.[20] The battle waged every year by the morality brigade as Valentine's Day approaches, threatening young couples against the Western import of romance, or a Mumbai Police commissioner telling men not to kiss their wives or girlfriends in public as this stokes crime, reflects a deeply conservative take on romance and sex.

This country has long been condemned to an endless journey of erotic barrenness, or 'sexual darkness' as the author and psychoanalyst Sudhir Kakar calls it.[21] Several intersecting reasons are attributed to this change, ranging from Muslim invasions, to the Victorian morality brought in by the British, and Gandhian puritanism, which valourizes the ideal man as a celibate or a *brahmachari*, who has insulated himself from women, reduced to sexual temptresses, and thereby protected his precious semen. And yet it was not always so.

Sexuality and Erotica – A Short History

Sexuality and erotica have been an integral part of Indian civilization, its culture and society. Though the idea of women and men interacting and developing romantic emotions is viewed by different countries differently, India has had a chequered history with love.

Love, translated into the Gandharva form of marriage is hailed by none other than Vatsyayana in the *Kama Sutra*, as the most superior form of marriage.[22] There is the rawness of the sensual, which is celebrated in so many dance forms, ranging from the classical Odissi (based on Jayadeva's poem 'Geet Govinda' celebrating the erotic play between Radha and Krishna), folk theatre forms like the popular *Lavani*, and folk songs which reflect regional sensibilities, including the undercurrents of passion and sexuality, which though camouflaged by an outward conservatism, is freely voiced through these folk traditions.

Many of them have a cross referencing of the *bhabhi-devar* or *jija-saali* relationship. Interestingly, some of them jettison the traditionally silenced sexuality of the woman to give her a voice, where in a mix of nuanced modesty, indignation, wit and need, she speaks to her lover and expresses her emotions as in this folk song from Bihar, which is often sung by women in spaces that are expunged of male presence. '*Alag ho ke soyo banne, mohe lage garmi, mohe lage garmi ki too hai bedardi* …' (Sleep away from me beloved, for I am feeling warm and you are too demanding).

In the iconoclastic documentary *Love in India*, the director Qaushiq Mukherjee or Q, unveils his own passionate relationship with his girlfriend set in sync with the parallel world of Radha and Krishna's *raas leela*, an eternal play of *shringar*. These erotic depictions of Krishna and Radha often appear in everyday places, which are somehow viewed as a form of divine play, not erotica. As a Janmashtami greeting, the day celebrating the birth of Krishna, I received a WhatsApp message from my office clerk – an intimate picture of Krishna caressing Radha's breast – a picture that the sender saw merely as a religious or artistic depiction. The Radha-Krishna iconography is a tribute to the fluidity of roles, where the lord is so often shown wooing his beloved with the tender humbleness of a lover – tying an anklet on her feet or hearing his flute from Radha's lips. These displays of sensuality in calendars, statues, miniature paintings etc. is an accepted part of religious iconography.

Given the interweaving of this thought process in our celebrated Indian culture, the repression of romantic love can only be counterproductive. It leads to a contradiction that gives confusing signals to the youth. How does one relate to a puritanical culture imposed as a top-down diktat and the strict control over women's behaviour, when the messages all around breathe of a freer, more liberal world? Perhaps it is this contrariness, the tensions created by opposing messages that make for the schizophrenic behaviour of some men towards women – worshipping goddesses and abusing the real women in their lives. On the obverse side, this lived lore of *raas* and romance has a positive aspect. It shows itself in the challenge that the young are posing to deeply entrenched social, cultural and caste divides.

Premarital Sex – A Survey

The survey, 'The Youth in India: Situation and Needs Study,' was conducted from 2004 to 2010. It was an ambitious project with 50,000 interviews conducted, that give us a window to one of the least talked about subjects: to what extent is premarital sex prevalent in the country. The findings are a revelation and debunk the general belief that there is very little premarital sex in the country. Instead we find that 15 per cent of unmarried young men and 4 per cent of unmarried young women reported engaging in sexual relations, mostly with a romantic partner. Though parents and family tried hard, the youngsters were able to form secret relationships. A significant number (21–23 per cent) said that they had been involved in a romantic partnership. 'Eighty-eight per cent of young men had held hands with a romantic partner, and 42 per cent had sex with their partner.' Among young women, while three-quarters had held hands with a romantic partner, just one in four (26 per cent) had engaged in sexual relations. The difference being that many of the interviewed men had engaged in sex with commercial sex workers or with older women.[23]

However, some contradictions do show up in the different surveys.[24,25,26] The Outlook–Karvy Insights Survey, conducted in the summer of 2019, across eight cities, including smaller towns like Kochi and Guwahati, show that some 80 per cent of the youth would like to get married someday;76 per cent oppose pre-marital sex and 50 per cent would like to ban porn sites. A sex survey by *India Today* (2019) shows that respondents in small towns are turning out to be as bold in their sexual choices as their big city counterparts, willing to experiment, fantasize and use medication like Viagra for enhanced pleasure.

Vitamin Stree, a young, video-first content platform shares the findings of an online sex survey done with 2,500 urban millennials aged between 18–35 years. It talked about everything from birth control and women's rights to pubic hair and body positivity. As revealed in the survey, majority of both men and women get information on sex before the age of 13, mostly from peers or from the internet, and watching porn seems to dominate their viewing pleasure with 91 per cent men and 63.4 per cent women admitting to consuming it. That translates to misinformation followed by misrepresentation, as their information on sex is skewed by the limited sources of information. Given such a scenario, women don't articulate enough about sex or pleasure ('no pain' is what most women associate with good sex) and men don't understand the nuances of the term 'consent'. Both sexes also don't lay enough emphasis on 'safe sex' as we shall discuss.

The unprecedented rural to urban migration has unleashed a huge churning process in the country. Education, jobs, freedom, economic possibilities, are a part of the treasure that the urban rainbow seems to beguile the less fortunate with. And they come in millions. Delhi and its NCR alone are facing a huge influx of migrants at practically two lakh migrants every year.[27] This story is repeated in cities and towns across the country. As people from differing cultures and value systems come to share spaces in the cities, the yawning gaps manifest their complexities. These are differences in backgrounds and social dynamics, such as caste, class, culture and attitudes to gender.

One has to step into the shoes of young men newly arrived in a city like Delhi, and employed as waiters in restaurants or in the thousands of beauty parlours mushrooming in the city, to understand their bafflement at what passes off as normal in the city as a contrast to the social behaviour in a village. Golu, 25 years old, came to Delhi after completing school and a few stints in various jobs in his hometown of Sitamarhi, a five-hour drive from the city of Patna. In Delhi, he found some odd jobs but then one of his relatives recommended that he get training in a beauty parlour, where the salary and the tips made for a tidy sum. Golu was so confused when he got to the parlour. In his hometown, women wearing shorts and showing off their bare skin was a part of youthful fantasies that they had seen only on screens. It shocked him at first, but then he realized that it was considered normal in Delhi. But his first training in giving a pedicure still stays as an abiding memory, that brought every conflicting idea under the scanner. In his village, men were not allowed to even come close to women, except their wives. And there he was, in that air-conditioned parlour, smearing cream on a woman's legs. Was she a loose woman? This is what he had learnt – to categorize women by certain behaviour patterns as 'good' women or 'bad' women. However, when he confided in his relative, a veteran in the industry, he laughed out loud at his naïve perception. That was a learning lesson for Golu – that certain forbidden behaviours in the village are acceptable in cities.

The same conflicting perceptions are at work with young women too. How are they supposed to interact with the opposite sex, what is safe behaviour – are all new and confusing questions for new migrants, without those claustrophobic restrictions that were part of their lives at homes. How free should one be on social media or whether to trust the man promising her the moon, are outside of their learned experience and therefore full of pitfalls. The media regularly reports about how the gullible fall for the lure set up by social media sites, where predators pose as empathetic friends. Similarly, the sudden loosening of social constraints for those still learning to negotiate the ways of the city can pose its own problems. Sexual exploration is an area laden with pitfalls for the inexperienced, as ignorance or carelessness towards precautions, can spiral into truly difficult situations. Senior Gynecologist Dr. Yuvakshi Juneja, practicing at a leading hospital in New Delhi, expresses her concern about young women and men, not taking adequate precautions. Frequent abortions or relying on the morning-after pill, has terrible effects on a woman's health. She's also concerned that men too are often irresponsible in their relationships and have multiple partners without using proper protection. In relationships, women sometimes fall into the trap of 'the man knows best' syndrome, when major decisions regarding safe sex are to be taken. This only exacerbates her vulnerability and sometimes abuse creeps into the relationship. This finding is corroborated on the ground too with an astounding lack of knowledge of sex and safe sex practices that the young have, as the SECRT study shows.[28] Few of the young women and men in the survey had information on sex and reproduction. Indeed, almost half of young women and one-sixth of young men reported that they had never received any information on sexual matters. Another survey reveals that an astounding 78 per cent of the respondents had practiced unprotected sex.[29] At least 63 per cent women had resorted to emergency contraceptives, with 16 per cent have done it nearly twice in the year. Consulting the doctor didn't feature in their orbit either, with 61 percent men and 51 percent women not visiting one, even when their health cried for one.

The state of flux is also giving rise to some dramatic relationships, with little stability or commitment. We see its manifestation in the rising tide of suicides, which are directly linked to the sorry carousel of jilted lovers and heartbreak. While a number of celebrities in these unfortunate situations get attention, there are many thousands of nameless lives, who meet the same fate under the same unfortunate circumstances. India has one of the highest youth suicide rates in the world with as many as [30] 20,000 of them in the 15-29 age group – around 15 per cent of the total number, caused by what is nearly a rite of passage for the young – heart break.

We also find a gradual change taking place in women's spaces. In her 1973 book *Love, Marriage and Sex*, the social scientist Promilla Kapur shows the change in the sexual norms among working women through a ten-year study. Kapur's target group was married and unmarried working Hindu women between the ages of twenty and forty years. She found that their attitudes towards sex had become more tolerant and liberal over the ten-year period. Qualifying her findings, she says, 'A greater number of these women now recognize sex as a great source of satisfaction in marriage, beside being a means of reproduction. The more open attitudes could be a reaction against the too rigid norms of a traditional society, or it might be the outcome of the need to appear more knowledgeable and modern in their attitudes towards sex.' The women interviewed in 1973 by Kapur have changed unrecognizably. The rapidly growing middle-class have higher aspirations for their daughters, particularly in urban India.

Here we share the views of young unmarried women from Kolkata and Delhi belonging to a privileged socio-economic class. Their choices are often bolstered by supportive parents, who try to balance the twin ends of encouraging their children's ambitions, while allaying their own anxieties about their marriage. The voices of these young women reflect a pragmatic and mature attitude, a clarity of thought and the will to carry through their choices. This group of twenty women were in their mid-twenties and were educated from English-medium schools. Eighty per cent of them were employed either in their own businesses or in the corporate world. They accepted that after marriage they would need to make adjustments, particularly if they were going to live in a joint family. They had no reservations about embracing the dynamics of their new family. However, reflecting a confidence that the generations before them could only dream about, they voiced the disclaimer – they would conform to the in-laws 'only if they respect me and will not take me for granted.' Ninety-nine per cent wished to marry for love. Distancing themselves from entrenched customs, they said, 'How can I marry a man when I don't know a thing about him?' And what are they looking for in a guy? To that question, the women reply that they want someone compatible. 'Looks are not the most important on the totem pole of wants, even money is not the biggest criteria, but yes, someone of an equivalent standard is needed.' Some were aware that getting the ideal man may not happen, in which case they would settle for an arranged marriage.

As social dynamics within India change and women are no longer seen as amputated from their parents' home after marriage, we asked: 'How involved would you like to be in your parental home after marriage?' 'Partially,' was the answer from some, while 40 per cent said, 'depending on whether I am in the same town or not.' The more idealistically inclined declared, 'There shouldn't be much change.' Though these surveys express the opinions from the more liberated sections of society, they do echo the emerging voices of young people everywhere. These are open, expressive of opinions and attitudes that will not be muzzled by the holy cows of tradition and specious arguments.

In many ways, love and its expression that challenges parental and societal approvals, have become a vocal form of protest against a closed society, that has for thousands of years sought to channel the course of emotions between women and men. An overwhelmingly young population is driving the change but the roadblocks remain, which in many ways echoes the many contradictions of this nation. Dynamic and on the move, yet thwarted by forces unwilling to let go of the static, young India is however reaching out for a world they wish to call their own.

6

THE DEVIL IS IN THE DOWRY

Back in the 1990s, an ad for Pan Parag, a pan masala, was aired regularly on TV. In a *shaadi ka ghar*, the bride's parents welcome the groom's parents for tea. Shammi Kapoor, an iconic Hindi film actor, declares with the authoritative flourish of the father of the bridegroom, '*Baraat theek aath baje pahunch jayegi. Par hum aapse ek baat to kehna bhool hi gaye!*' He pauses while the bride's father, played by another Hindi film legend Ashok Kumar, exchanges alarmed looks with his wife, worried if there are any demands for dowry coming their way. This ad played on several tropes that define the arranged marriage system; most specifically that the boy's family would voice their demands and the bride's parents would have to fulfil them. The ad had a happy ending though – the *baraatis* demanded to be welcomed with Pan Parag. It's all very light-hearted and delightful, but in reality, dowry remains the unfortunate reality that casts its degrading and demeaning shadow over many Indian weddings.

What do Women Inherit?

But how has it taken these Frankensteinian dimensions, an unwanted guest threatening to disrupt the wedding celebrations?

To demystify the layered complexity of the dowry system, we need to first understand the custom of *streedhan*, its evolvement, and its gradual degeneration into naked avarice as we know it today.

To understand it comprehensively, we also need to delve into patriarchy and the division of wealth amongst the sons and daughters in a family. Those familiar with the traditional patriarchal setup, wouldn't find this statement confounding. Because largely, patriarchy works to safeguard the interest of the males, it's men who inherit the money-making assets – real estate, agriculture land, the family business, the fixed deposits, shares and bonds, etc. It's pretty much an unsaid assumption that after the death of the parents the sons would inherit whatever is left behind. If there is a daughter in the same family, what is given to her is also fairly predictable.

But before we come to the brass tacks of inheritance, we must acknowledge that one of the biggest goals for parents is to get their daughter married and so far as possible, to marry her off well. And how is this translated, besides getting a good match for her? Fancy, lavish weddings belong to the upper crust of the society, but amongst the middle-classes too, a wedding would include the must-haves – the *shamiaana* festooned with lights, a DJ, elaborate feasts, special clothes and jewellery, and of course, the bride's trousseau, along with a new wardrobe, jewellery, some furniture, a car perhaps, electronics, utensils, cash, fixed deposits and other gifts.

Into this expense account, are also added the gifts given to her husband during the wedding ceremonies, money in case they have bargained for it and also the plethora of gifts for her in-laws. This portion of the parental wealth, mostly movable, called *dahej* in North India, is given to the daughters of the house.

The gift-giving often begins from the time of the engagement, when cash, sweets and other gifts are given to the groom's side in order to honour them. Honouring them is a deeply entrenched social process where the 'bride taker' is seen as having the upper hand in the power equation. So, it follows that the bride's family has no expectations of getting any gifts in return, though the bride herself might receive some. This giving of gifts by the bride's family continues or is at least expected to stretch over a lifetime of ceremonies and festivals, extending to the time when her own children get married. These obligations convey a nuanced variation of love and kinship, honouring her as the daughter of the house, while a subtle message of separateness from her parental home is also underlined. Despite the skewed male bias in large swathes of the society, the daughter inhabits a very special space, a deep symbiotic connection, but this is seen as different from the son's.

So how is this transition from the sentimental to the material seen in real terms? In many ways the dowry is the woman's financial inheritance. And yet this financial handover by the parents has come under the lens and earned huge negative publicity. Does that mean that a woman should not be given these gifts as she leaves her parents' home?

The Dowry Defined

To set the context, we need to return to the traditional understanding of the difference between *dahej* (dowry)[1] and *streedhan*.[2]

Dowry, according to the *Collins Dictionary* is the money or property brought by a woman to her husband at marriage. A disclaimer in italics accompanies the meaning: 'now chiefly historical or metaphorical'. The Indian Penal code defines dowry as a 'direct or indirect deal' demanded by the groom or his family. From here on it became a loaded term, superimposed by the imagery of the gluttonous, demanding and coercive groom or his family. There is that ominous threat, which accompanies these demands like a malevolent cloud – give in or else! What is the 'or else', but a warning entwined into the unequal relations between the husband and the wife, that a regressive section of society still follows and believes in.

Streedhan, literally means stree (woman) and dhan (her wealth). The law has extensive references to what is exactly meant by *streedhan*, with commentaries made under the *Mitakshara* and *Dayabagha* system, with quotes from Manu and Yajnavalkya and other sages who have laid down what a woman should inherit. *Streedhan* is a voluntary gift given by members of the bridal side to the bride as a stepping stone to establishing her own property. It is property, gifts, etc. that are given to a woman without 'demand, coercion, undue influence or even pressure'. In its contemporary interpretation, it would mean that the woman has full right over the disposal of the properties considered *streedhan*. The Hon'ble Supreme Court of India held that: 'A Hindu married woman is the absolute owner of her *Streedhan* property and can deal with it in any manner she likes and, even if it is placed in the custody of her husband or her in-laws they would be deemed to be trustees and bound to return the same if and when demanded by her'.

But as social practices went into a downward spiral of demand and coercion, the wealth given to women has devolved into the ugliness of the dowry. There are different theories to give us an insight into how this happened – that an empowering tool like *streedhan* transformed into the greedy, humiliating and sometimes fatal avatar of dowry. Historian and anthropologist Veena Talwar

Oldenberg, who conducted a prodigious 15 years of research on the subject, even delving into the paper trail left by the British, has a different take on the subject of dowry, which she says is subsumed under the concept of *streedhan*. I quote from her book: *Dowry Murder: The Imperial Origins of a Cultural Crime*[3] to provide an understanding of the contemporary discourse on dowry and its distorted legacy, by fusing the present with historical practices skewed by the British Machiavellian mechanisms. Veena writes: 'In precolonial times dowry was not a problem,' but a support for women, a mark of their social status and safety net.' She demonstrates through arguments and research that 'dowry and the wedding expenses neither caused the impoverishment of the Punjab peasant, which is what early colonial administrators claimed, nor did it cause increase in violence against women whether in the form of female infanticide or today's bride burning. Rather imperial policies created a more masculine economy and deepened the preference for sons that fostered the overt act of killing of girls ... To ensure against the political dangers of intrusive social reforms, the East India Company sought native participation in framing the crime as a cultural product.' She goes on to add that the East India Company initially formed to conduct only trade, having tasted the riches of the country once it managed to wrest the revenue in the 'conquered province of Bengal in 1765,' it continued with its 'aggressive empire building' (that) led to the conquest of Punjab in 1849 and later Oudh in 1856. The Company needed to make a compelling case to defend its ruthless actions and policies of expansion, to a critical British Parliament and the British public by making a case for its 'civilizing mission' amongst uncivilized 'Hindu cultural practices'. It therefore immediately yoked the practice of female infanticide (which was practiced across various high and low caste Hindu communities, Sikhs and Muslims, and communities that paid bride price instead of dowry, as a crude method of ensuring more males, but was not linked to dowry) to the giving of dowry. They made community elders pledge against the practice and in one stroke demolished a major economic and social citadel for women.

She continues, 'the dowry demands complained about in the 1960s were non-existent in 1867. There is no evidence in this period that the groom's family could demand specific consumer goods or large amounts of money', instead dowry mostly comprised of a voluntary giving of clothes, jewellery, cash etc. it is emphatically seen as a matter of honor for the groom's side to accept what is given as a dowry to the bride'. In forty-nine separate volumes of customary law in an equal number of districts of colonial Punjab – which include present day Haryana, Jammu, Himachal Pradesh and Delhi as well – 'it was this idea of dowry that was accepted. But in the aftermath of the massive economic and societal upheaval brought on by imperial rule, women's entitlements to the precious resources obtained from land were erased and their control of the system diminished, ultimately resulting in a devaluing of their very lives.'

The introduction of the Ryotwari System forever changed the tiller's relationship to land. It fixed land revenue payments and modified property rights to give male members the titular ownership of land, so that '*they could be taken to court or sent to jail*' if they defaulted on revenue payments. 'Putting landed property in male hands exclusively and holding the males responsible for payment of revenue had the effect of creating the Indian male as the dominant legal subject; this happened throughout British India and even in the independent Princely states...Sons would inherit and be in charge, and their widowed mothers would be their dependents-at-will; women who had no sons would have no rights and would become dependent on the charity of their stepsons or the husband's other agnatic kin'.

These ominous changes were further exacerbated by the typical imperial policy to build its military from the local populace. The British created huge employment opportunities by recruiting the robust Punjabi males (mostly Jats) in the military. During 'hard times created by the revenue policies that generated money to pay for them, a military career brought the peasant family the security that had been compromised by making its lien on land so tenuous.' These policies in effect engineered a masculine economy. The preference for sons deepened leading to 'gender targeting', which was achieved through female infanticide. With that the definition of dowry changed irrevocably from being a voluntary safety net, into a pernicious practice buoyed by greed and demand, where the groom's family bargained for money and land, with the hope of bolstering their own resources and thereby guarding themselves against the economic penury that British policies had reduced them to.

'The landscape changed, its deleterious impact scarring the land to this day. What was once a relationship based society was converted to a contract based society by applying capitalistic ideas (individual land rights), importing British prejudices (crippling women's rights) and advancing colonial motives (discrediting Hindu culture to justify civilizing mission)'.

While this view is provocative and could have many counter arguments[4] to it, what remains incontrovertible is that women used to enjoy their right to *streedhan*. But as the patriarchal noose became tighter and women's social position was lowered, the need to give a woman economic autonomy became less urgent. Instead the focus shifted to giving gifts in accordance to the wish list furnished by her in-laws, and over which she barely had a shared claim.

Given that we are living in times of the market economy, dowry has become the economic fulcrum around which the foundation of marriage is built; a bargaining tool, used as a bait in the traditional arranged marriage setup. Post the matching of castes, a girl's other qualifications such as looks, complexion, education, household skills, etc., are all add-ons, after the primary conditions of the scale of the wedding and the size of the dowry are met. With this thought process, the matchmakers or brokers in an arranged marriage, consider it perfectly normal and valid to initiate the conversation by asking the girl's family, 'So how much are you going to spend?' This one answer determines the future course of affairs.

Brokering a marriage is considered an entirely legitimate deal in certain business communities, where marriage alliances are forged based on the money the girl's side is ready to fork out. A lavish destination wedding on a Greek island or in Bali or Phuket, with all expenses borne by the girl's family is not seen as a quantum jump in demands, but is accepted with an almost touching humbleness by the boy's family. Different communities have their own ceremonies during the course of the wedding, when the bride's side sends numerous trays laden with gifts and boxes of mithai to honour the bridegroom's side. In more modest families, who form the vast middle-classes of the country, where income and aspirations leave meagre savings, a laundry list of demands often result in bleeding bank balances, debt and a burning resentment. The helpless submission to the groom's demands and shrinking money reserves, directly impacts the bride-to-be. The narrative that probably runs like a ticker tape in their head is along these line – 'we have a daughter, we are lower to them so we have to do whatever it takes to please the boy's side.' In a family of multiple unmarried daughters, the reality is an anxiety-laden trial where their future, their marriage and the burden of their dowry, becomes a part of 'liability' that they need to cater to.

Such normalized gender discrimination is evident when a man equates his financial status with the perks of his job, his bank balance, property owned and an earning son, while an unmarried daughter, whether or not she is earning an income, is labelled a liability. What is missing in this picture is that in a comparison of expenditures, we don't give enough thought to the amount of money spent on a son's education, which often exceeds that spent on the daughter.

'Missing' Girls

This dystopia, where the sex of a child determines its value and economic worthiness, has led to a country with some of the most skewed sex ratios in the world.[5] According to the last census, the number of girls in the 0-6 years category has dropped dramatically, and as per the Economic Survey 2017-2018, the government of India admits to a situation where we have some 63 million girls 'missing',[6] an euphemism for the most dastardly of crimes – female foetuses systematically aborted. The signs are everywhere. In a hospital when a baby girl arrives, the nurse and doctors announce it with a moroseness that spells of a family tragedy, while a boy's entry into the world comes amidst toothy smiles and the distribution of laddoos. Across 132 villages in Himachal Pradesh, in just 3 months in 2019, there were 216 births but not a single girl was born – a natural disaster or a manmade horror, the answer is not too far to seek.[7]

Parneeti a young woman, all of twenty-four years old, was expecting her second child when I met her. She lives in Gurugram, the technical and commercial hub of Haryana. Her life had followed the typical trajectory of a middle-class girl married at the age of twenty, having finished high school and no job skills. Her husband was employed as an office peon in an MNC located in the bustling commercial hub. She lived with her in-laws in a two-room flat in the cheaper part of the town. While talking to me, there was a desperation in her eyes as she looked at her 3-year-old daughter playing in the school courtyard, where I had gone to meet her. She recounted how her mother-in-law, had forced her earlier to abort her female foetus, despite the government clamp down on foetal sex determination. 'How did she find out?' I asked. 'Oh, there are many ways, like bribe the staff. Of course, it can be done. But now I am so worried, if it's a girl I will have to abort it again. Or my sasuraal will throw me out. Every night in bed my husband only talks about having a son, and what he dreams for him.'

From Parneeti's two-room low-income housing to a plush five-bedroom apartment in Mumbai's swanky Malabar Hills, the story in unchanged except for some superficial details. Neeta and her husband Rajesh were planning to go to Singapore on a mission. Three years into their marriage and with a baby daughter, it was time to have a second baby but this time it had to be a boy. Having money meant that they didn't have to leave desire to the whimsy of chance. The couple planned to go for artificial insemination, where Neeta would be implanted with a 'male' sperm. Neeta is now six months pregnant. She shared the travails of the process where it went wrong twice. They had injected a 'female' sperm and that had to be rejected. She was now expecting her baby boy in a few months. Her father-in-law had promised her a BMW at the birth, Neeta shared with the slightest hint of remorse in her eyes. Such stories lie at the very core of the systematic disappearance of the girl child, much like an endangered species dashing towards extinction.

Dowry and its far-reaching fallouts, bolster the argument that globalization and development in its holistic sense have a long way to go before the gender scripts woven into the Indian psyche begin to unravel.[8,9]

The Groom is King

The mythology of marriage continue to valorize the male. The groom's side is the *maan daan*, literally those who need to be revered. This recognition of the superior side versus the subordinated bride's side, who are responsible for the obsequious hospitality, plays itself out in a very conscious expression of their roles during the wedding. While khatirdari is a singular aspect of it, what becomes highly suspect is when the groom's side insists on translating the hospitality into material wants. Though this falls short of the shameless avarice of dowry demands, it is equally reprehensible.

To some extent, love marriages have bucked the trend, with parents who have not been instrumental in finding the bride or groom, now accommodating the choices of their children in the wedding arrangements. Here dowry certainly takes a backseat if not entirely rejected. This connection between love marriages and no dowry might have a pattern though.

In an informal discussion held with ten young men, who were graduates or held professional degrees; living in dormitory style accommodation in a congested hub of Delhi, I asked the question: 'Arranged or love marriage, what is your choice?' The men worked in different kinds of jobs in the private sector. Some were management trainees, a couple of them were working in the IT sector, some with NGOs etc., their income ranging between ₹25-40 thousand per month. Except for a couple of them, most chimed that they were uncomfortable with the idea of a love marriage. 'Why?' 'My parents will not like it,' they said though they declared that they themselves had nothing against it. One of them harboured the notion that a love marriage would mean one was already too familiar with the woman and that would make things predictable. Some even let their guard down enough to say that it was okay to have a 'good time' with a girl but for marriage they would go with their parents' choice. On further probing, it emerged that the men felt that going for a love marriage would mean that they would be deprived of a dowry. Many of them felt that getting a dowry was necessary to their well-being. Some claimed that they had taken education loans that needed to be paid back. Others said they needed to set up their home in case they had to move out, while others declared that the dowry received by them would establish their worth in concrete terms. The two men who had not agreed with the arranged marriage chorus were already in relationships.

A sociologist working with a non-profit put these attitudes into perspective. She felt that many young men were unwilling to take responsibility for their actions, and enthralled by a more consumerist society keep dowry as a central consideration in chalking out their future plans.[10] This certainly seemed to reflect the arrested growth of many young men, who, instead of taking responsibility for their actions, adopted a juvenile dependency in seeking the lollipops that came their way in the form of dowry.

To go beyond the lena dena, to understand how a woman looks at the giving of dowry, would help us get a glimpse into the deep scars it leaves behind. Even though its repeated practice has made most people inured to it. And yet from all accounts it is deeply humiliating for a woman, where she feels herself treated like a commodity. Her sense of worth and self-respect is deeply compromised when a man refuses to marry her unless the dowry demands are met. It's an in-your-face ignominy that all her achievements, her education or even her looks come to naught and her parents reduced to supplicants trying to get the groom's parents to consider their daughter. Grooms of course come with price tags. Social status, education, job, and to some extent physical features, determine what the bride's family have to pay to get the match going.

My neighbour's domestic helper, earning ₹20,000 a month, is facing a demand of ₹8 lakhs as dowry for her daughter's wedding. The prospective groom is working in a contractual job with the government. The tentacles of the system writhe in insidious ways when marriage is on the cards. Meera who writes a blog called meerareflections says: 'The marriage market in India is a strange place—it is a seller's market but the commodity sold does not become the property of the buyer! Men are prime property in this market. There is literally a "price" that they command. So, a girl would still have to pay the "market price" to be able to marry a "decent" man. This situation is further complicated by the fact that all marriages are endogamous within one's own caste—a girl's family either pays or the girl stays unmarried.'[11]

The Search for the Elusive Groom

The patriarchal gaze is the deeply insidious working of gender roles during a traditional wedding. The entire twist of culture, economics, tradition, caste and hypergamy, where a girl steps up on the status ladder through marriage, conspires to establish that the groom's family is inevitably superior.

It is this mindset, which twists the narrative in favour of the male, despite the demographic dividend which should have turned the script in favour of the girls. Considering the terrifying sex ratio, it is baffling why there is a dearth of eligible males when the matchmaking process is put into motion.

That probably is the inherent anomaly which often escapes the eye – because when looking for a man higher up on the status ladder – superior or equal to the bride's family on various parameters, the numbers dwindle because as we go higher up the class ladder, the families are getting smaller. There are not enough men armed with all the attributes that the girl's families seek. However, when the tables are reversed and the guys go looking for girls, the pool is bigger because the list of requirements is shorter. For e.g., it doesn't matter whether the girl lives in a joint family, the town she is from, her job or career prospects, etc. Because a woman is expected to jettison her unmarried life completely and adapt to her husband's life and home.

But as Ratna Chadha, who heads Tirun Travels, asks indignantly, 'why do families always look for marrying their daughter into a family that is supposedly higher in the social stakes? What is it that our girls lack that they need to depend on a man to look after her? Today we have trained our daughters to the point where they have everything – money, education, independence, the freedom to move where they want and they are also perfectly capable of earning for themselves. They don't need a man to look after them? She just wants a man with whom she has compatibility.' Ratna has a point there, that perhaps if more women had a wealth cache to inherit or at least fall back on in adversity, then women's families would not be so desperately looking for a man to support her.

We also need to ask why does the bride's family need to provide a dowry? The question strikes at the very root of unequal power equations, but the anthropologist Ursula Sharma adds an economic angle to it.[12] She talks about this giving of goods in terms of pure economics. While the sons earn an income, the woman would not be contributing directly to the economic wealth of the family. Hence, to compensate for a non-performing member who is viewed to be an economic liability, compensation is sought. This theory only reinforces the argument propagated by academics involved in women studies – that women's unpaid work is not enumerated and therefore her immense but unaccounted for contribution to the household is ignored. This gives further credence to Ratna's argument of financial independence as an empowering tool that can free women from the worst syndromes of dependency.

The Right to Inherit

Disinheriting daughters from the material wealth of their parental home has wide-ranging ripple effects. Wedding expenses and gifts for a girl cannot be seen as an accepted form of being a conscience saver for the parents, with her brothers monopolizing the inheritance. What fosters this mindset? Age-old gender biases that lead to equally biased behaviour. Prof. Bina Agarwal in her research has shown how notions of family and tradition are used to deprive women from what should be her right. She mentions an incident which shows how even State actors are equally guilty of maintaining the domination of the male and afraid to alter this fundamental power equation. When she asked the agricultural minister responsible for bringing reforms to correct the anomalies of inheritance, the male minister replied with suitable ire, 'Are you suggesting that women be given rights in land? What do women want? To break the family?'[13] Most men would agree with the minister's divisive rhetoric, while some women would hesitate to question the dynamics of power and inheritance. They too have been conditioned to believe their diminished importance in their natal home.[14]

Which also brings us to the prospect of what happens to the wealth of an unmarried daughter – who inherits it, who stands to gain from it? According to Sections 14, 15 and 16 of the Hindu Succession Act, 1956, there is no distinction made between a married and unmarried woman regarding the disposal of her property and other assests and follows the same order of devolvement amongst her relatives.

The traditional beliefs of inequality come from certain rituals like kanyadaan. This is one of the most regressive Hindu wedding customs, causing endless heartbreak among women and their families, where a girl is 'donated' or 'gifted' by the parents to the husband – a transference of belonging, which effectively severs her from the parental home. Manu, the ancient lawmaker had mentioned this form of the marriage rite as one of the eight forms that were in practice, but the pandit-led patriarchal norms have continuously pumped up its primacy in the wedding ceremony. In Tamil Nadu, many modern families are shunning the kanyadaanam as a regressive ritual preferring instead the ritual of panigraham, but the sentiment behind it remains practically unchanged. Usually, the bride is made to sit on the father's lap who gives her away to the groom, a symbolic gesture entrusting him with her responsibility. These practices reinforce the 'paraya dhan' sentiment of a woman, that runs like a fault line in everyday conversations, movies and literature of the country. Sons, on the other hand, are the permanent keepers of ancestral pride, property and lineage. Women could of course can lay claim to their share of parental property under the Hindu Succession law, with a few caveats. But mostly they don't.

At the core of this silencing, lies the psychological priming through childhood and adolescence, including rituals and religious festivals, telling girls about sacrifice and renunciation as befitting a woman. Sometimes parents too make short shrift of such ambitions. While the daughter/sister is not only entitled to her share of her parental property but also to a share that her husband inherits from his family. An unfair double scoop, say the conservative traditionalists.

But changing times call for new ways of looking at a woman's role in the family. Education and a career have empowered her to play a more active role in interacting with her parents even after marriage, with many taking care of their aging parents. The fallacious argument that the son alone will look after the parents in their old age, is being rubbished in middle-class families across the country. This shift is forcing families to examine their attitudes towards their daughters and sons, particularly in the distribution of the wealth.

A dinner table discussion involving a group of women and men, who belonged to wealthy business families, was focussed on the burning question of the day: what part of one's wealth should one give to the daughter? The question was anchored around the notion of the son as the inheritor and the eventual owner of the business, along with the acknowledgment that a girl should be given her fair share too. In the past such a question would not have ever raised its head but today it does. The answer is a no brainer. Train women to run businesses as you train your sons. Give her the property to call her own, let inheritance be fair and equitable, empower her so she can be the master of her own fate.

Undisguised Greed

A horrific repercussion of disinheritance is spectre of dowry and the endless exploitation of women because of it. The dowry demanders see her as the golden goose, who must be squeezed for all her worth to pay for their wildest fantasies and every material dream, while at the same time treating her like she is worth almost nothing. News stories of the most bizarre dowry demands, accompanied by harrowing tales of humiliation and abuse, are almost as a daily occurrence, with many times their number going unreported. There is no predictable pattern to this greed and demand. Sometimes the claim is made before the wedding and stops with it, but at times it can continue for years, where the threat of sending the woman back to her parental home, or torture and humiliation become the pressure points for the extraction. It's at this point that parents need to take a call and bring her back or approach the courts, but much of India still balks at the idea of having a daughter 'returned'. 'What will the people say?' is a constant refrain in many homes. Aishwarya, a young woman shared this story about her 28-year-old roommate, who is living as a paying guest with her in Noida and looking for a job. 'My friend left her husband, fed up with his beatings and violence. His family was always asking for something or the other – a new TV, microwave, then jewellery during Diwali and now cash as they wanted to buy a new flat. Finally, her parents refused and that made him even more angry. But she can't go back to her parents either. Her father says, "We have married you off, our responsibility is over. Now it is for you to stay at your sasuraal, the in-laws, whether they beat you or humiliate you, we can't do anything more."'

Anguished by this parental helplessness, activists want to know 'why did the parents not intervene, how could they shut their eyes to the torture and the humiliation of their daughter who is their flesh and blood? Why did they ask her to stay in that hell hole with that husband? If they can come up after her death to allege torture by her husband and in-laws, why did they do nothing while she was alive?' Which also brings us to the other question: why do girls not speak up when dowry demands are made before their wedding and they know how much it troubles the parents? And what is it that even educated girls lack that makes them put up with the humiliations and the trauma brought on by this practice? The answers lie at the root of our social conditioning: the lessons we teach our girls and the messages they themselves imbibe from their surrounding world. If she is told from her childhood that marriage is her goal and her dharma, and the husband's home her ultimate destiny, where she has to stay no matter what happens, we back her into a corner where she sees her unhappiness and her kismet as two sides of the coin. Madhu Kishwar and Ruth Vanita express this socialisation process in greater detail, giving perspective to the abuse by a mother-in-law over her daughter-in-law, within the context of dowry demands, where horrific acts committed by the former have been reported.[15] What motivates this abusive cruelty in an otherwise, presumably normal woman? The answer can perhaps be found in the realms of psychology, where much like those subjected to violence and abuse, perpetrate it on others when in positions of power. The mother-in-law who has been degraded, beaten and insulted her whole life, finally gets to disgorge the accumulated poison of her own abuse on her helpless daughter-in-law. Perhaps the first person who is lower than her in the family hierarchy. A woman has been taught to think of this torture as 'normal', a 'woman's fate'. Religion, films, her elders, her own and her mother's experience, all tell her that if a woman is unhappy, nothing can be done about it. It is her own fault.

Back in the 1970s, when there was a spate of deaths of mostly young, newly-married women, the deaths attributed to burn injuries caused by the bursting of stoves, civil society and women's groups refused to be cowed down by the facile explanations provided by the police. These deaths came to be known as dowry deaths.[16] Activists have given a graphic account of their encounter with a family that had murdered a young bride, Tarvinder Kaur, 24 years old in 1979, because she had failed to get a scooter for her husband.[17] Despite her dying statement, the police had recorded the death as suicide. The authors vividly describe the demonstration they helped organize outside the man's house in a bid to name and shame them and the hostility they faced from the neighbours, who were fiercely angry at this unwanted interference by outsiders, in what they saw as a family matter.

The Dowry Prohibition Act 1961 was amended in 1984 and again in 1986. While it had some stringent provisions for punishing offenders, dowry deaths continued unabated. In 1991, there were 91 reported cases of death of women by stoves bursting and an astounding 4,800 complaints of torture in dowry-related cases. Considering that the vast number of cases are buried under a system that believes that the 'ghar ki izzat' should not be compromised by reporting to the police, one can only imagine the monumental numbers of such cases that go unreported. Despite legislation and a media-fanned awareness, dowry deaths continue to be a reality in our country. In April 2016, Maneka Gandhi, Minister of Women and Child Affairs, declared in the parliament that in the last three years, as many as 24,771 women had died as a result of dowry.

A senior lawyer with a law firm in Delhi that specialises in dowry cases, shared a story of her client as an example of how even educated girls fall into the dowry trap. She mentions the case of Dipa, from a middle-class business family, who during her courtship had often heard her fiancé sharing his great dream of going to Malaysia and Thailand for their honeymoon. While he didn't have the money to fund such a trip, it didn't dampen his desire. The obliging girl then pestered her parents into paying for this honeymoon package, which they managed only after selling off a family property. That turned out to be only the beginning of a nightmare, as his demands went on and on. 'He just wouldn't stop, and when he didn't get the cash or whatever he was asking for, he would turn violent and abusive,' the lawyer shared. Until finally Dipa left him after two years of being in an abusive marriage. And that is how the senior lawyer was fighting her case.

A Case for Women Having Their Own Wealth

In India, only 26 per cent women are employed, which comprises both the formal and the informal economy (2018), which is abysmally low when compared to all other developing countries in the region.[18] We have seen that women rarely get to inherit family wealth. With her participation in the job market at such low levels too, it follows that the sense of empowerment which comes with financial independence, remains an elusive longing for the average Indian woman. A clutch of reasons lie behind this glaring inequality in labour force participation, as I have explored in my book *Women's Working World – A Mirror to Their World*. Gender roles, the attitudes of in-laws who don't want a working bahu are only a part of the problem. As a senior HR consultant working with Wipro, one of India's leading IT companies said at a seminar on the subject, 'Attrition rates are really high amongst women with nearly 70 per cent of them quitting their job once they get married. The rest leave when the children arrive. Of course, we hope that with longer maternity leave, women will get back to work.' What emerges is a mindset, where the woman's primary role is seen as being the caregiver.

In an interview, Indra Nooyi, the former CEO of PepsiCo, narrated an incident when she was made president on the board of directors of the company, a high point of her career. She went home early to share the news with her family, but her mother ignored the news and instead asked her to get some milk for the morning.[19] Indra's indignation with her mother's indifference to her achievements is retold as an story of women's lives, and is particularly pertinent to the Indian context. Patriarchy endorses this caretaker role wholeheartedly, projecting all women to be virtuous and dutiful in their many roles to serve others first. Most men and even some women are uncomfortable with women who have professional aspirations, and mitigate this discomfort by belittling her achievements, trivializing her efforts or by branding her as a power-hungry battle axe. 'Neglecting her family!' is another potent allegation levelled at her, which addles many career women with guilt. Hence, a large majority of them quit full-time work once they are married and have kids. At least everyone else is happy, she tells herself, while trying to assuage her own frustration.

If dowry was meant to be a tool to ease her life, it certainly doesn't seem to be serving its purpose anymore. Considering the interminable abuse and discrimination that result from it, why do we still have this practice? We, of course, understand it as an economic exchange, which is used to further the interests of different groups within the family. In north India, property is normally seen as belonging to the whole family, even though the patriarchal head makes all the decisions and sometimes allots the fruits of one person's labour to other members of the family. Sharma points out that power structures in the normal family is defined by age and gender.[20] The elders get respect from the juniors and the women defer to the men. The bride certainly has no or little say in how her property is to be used. But older women, once they enter the system, begin to voice their opinions of this economic exchange. In their new roles as mother and mother-in-law, its they who decide on how the dowry is to be given for her daughter, and how it is to be used in the case of her son.[21]

Preeti, a woman in her fifties had thrown a lavish wedding in a 5-star hotel for her daughter a year before our interview, tried to make me understand why she had given really extravagant gifts to the in-laws, 'I did not give dowry but really went overboard giving gifts to the whole family. The whole shebang, so that the in-laws would be really impressed ... to keep them happy, so that they too keep my daughter happy when she goes to their house. They will also say that she comes from a good family, which has good values. That is what made me go the whole hog.'

We have heard the mother's side of the story but how about the father, what are his thoughts about the daughter's marriage? Given the socialization processes, from the time a daughter is born, fathers do feel a special sense of responsibility, which is finally fulfilled once she's married. Through the various stages of her life – adolescence, the teenage years and then on to adulthood, each stage signals different responsibilities for him, and through it all marriage looms as the big destination point. He does feel responsible for keeping aside enough money to get her married well. Articulating this popular pulse, many advertisements for banks use 'emotional father with daughter as bride' imagery. But encouragingly, a daughter's education too is becoming a priority that parents are now saving for.

I happened to be talking to a group of about ten employees working in a foreign embassy in Delhi. Since their ex-ambassador's spouse was with us, they were eager to share how well they were living the middle-class dream since her departure nearly five years back. The talk instinctively veered towards their children and their occupations. Some of the men, not unusually, began talking about their sons and their achievements; how well they were doing in their studies, and how they were poised to step into successful careers as engineers, or a dentist, management trainees, etc. The fathers bristled with enviable pride as they spoke about their boys. I turned to another man Maniram, who had been silent the whole time, looking a little left out of the glory stakes. 'Well, he has three daughters,' someone tried to explain helpfully. Unexpectedly, the man perked up visibly, as if he had thought of some achievement that he could now share. He announced with some satisfaction that his eldest daughter had just got married. I ignored that and asked more directly, 'But what has she done?' And the man replied, 'Arre, I have completed my biggest responsibility – she's married. What more do I have to think about?' The others nodded in silent collusion – yes, this too was a part of the middle-class dream.

It would be delusional to imagine that this belief system is limited only to those from the lower income groups. I have discovered in my interactions across classes, that certain concerns run along predictable lines. Whilst talking to a senior government employee, he spoke feelingly about having just accomplished the task of getting his daughter married. 'I am so relieved she's gone to her home while I am still in service,' he said with fervid candour, trying to mask it under the hauteur of an IAS officer.

Changing Mindsets – A Silver Lining

The scenario is not entirely bleak though. Many women and men refuse to give or take dowry, some even declaring that they would not take anything beyond the customarily auspicious ₹1 in the form of a blessing. Several surveys show that women do not approve of giving dowry. It's a sentiment, which could help to slowly change the attitudes of the family too, given that older women have a central role to play in the weddings of their sons.

Media images, popular culture, exposure to social media, education, financial independence and the changed perception of the parents too, have made women declare: 'I want to break free!' It's given women the courage to walk out of nightmarish conditions and chalk new lives. There are new sections in the law that support and strengthen women, and offer her protection. Having a job and a wallet filled with one's own hard-earned cash gives a tremendous boost to one's self-image. All of these contribute to making women confident and self-aware by the time they step into the wedding market.

One could cite the case of Alka, coming from an average family of Gorakhpur, who had clawed her way into becoming an engineer and later got a job in Infosys, one of the country's largest IT companies. There was even the chance of her going for a training stint to the US. But her mother was hell-bent on getting her married before that, with the grandmother adding to the pressure too. Finally, a suitable boy, an engineer, was found. But there was a hitch, when the boy's father said with a smile, 'We want ten lakhs cash to settle our son.' While people rarely expect the prospective bride to confront her in-laws on such an issue, Alka not only accused her fiancé of being greedy but called the wedding off. The boy approached her again, promising that his father would never repeat the demand again. Alka, under pressure from her parents and family, finally agreed to the marriage. When all the preparations for the marriage were in place and the baraat was at the door, the father again demanded ten lakhs in cash, sanguine in the belief that on the verge of the wedding and amidst the presence of their relatives, the girl's side would have no alternative but to give the money. But they really hadn't factored in Alka's determination, who on hearing of the renewed demand, shed her bridal coyness and stepped out to meet the baraat, where she shamed the two publicly by sharing their story of greed and manipulation. For good measure, her father called the cops as well and the two were booked for a criminal offence.

The social narrative of the country is an interweaving of historical biases and a cultural understanding of the place it accords to its women and men, coloured at least for the last two decades by relentless consumerism fueled by a market economy. A condition where all the chips have been unfairly stacked. The winning hand belonging to patriarchy and its precepts! But a change is taking place with defiant voices that are getting louder and gathering momentum against a lopsided system. Alka's is not an isolated voice nor her case entirely unique. Yet what gives hope for the future is that we now have the conditions where women like Alka can stand up against endemic injustice, and there are other voices supporting her across mainstream media, the social media, and most hearteningly within her own family.

7

THE SINGULAR LIFE: MARRIAGE FROM THE OTHER SIDE

The belief that marriage is an inevitable rite of passage, an essential life event for all humans, as some believe and preach with a missionary zeal, is attracting a volley of opposing views today. The world is no longer ruled by absolutes. The idea of the permanent is disappearing. Changing climates, social mobility, moving populations – the conjugation of the economic and the socio-cultural is really the story of our times. Individualism, once seen as an undesirable Western trait, is becoming the reality of India's youth as well. Relationships are becoming more fluid. And marriage as an institution is competing with other forms of relationships, which are certainly less formal, that is when it is not being dismissed entirely by a growing tribe of singles.

India, the Queen of Contradictions

India has always lived up to its label of being the 'queen of contradictions', defying the black and white from ancient times. While marriage continues to be an important aspiration for many, there is the other side too. The non-conformists never have it easy though; cooperation and coercion is often used for convincing the obstinate. Even though in Hindu philosophy there is deep reverence for *brahmacharya*, or the celibate – whose practitioners have learnt to control their sexual instinct and by extension the senses, an intrinsic element for the spiritually enlightened. But this contradiction, like in most ancient philosophies, with so much emphasis on *kama* as one of the *purusharthas*, is equally puzzling. Brahmacharya [1] exhorts the spiritual seekers to not only abstain from sexual activity, but to refuse the desire to even pop in one's head. The ancient treatise calls it the state of retaining the seminal fluid, the vital force that energises the spiritual path.

Sri Swami Sivanada, one of the foremost yoga masters and Vedanta gurus of the twentieth century, in his book *Practice of Brahamacharya*, goes into great detail about its huge potency and the reasons why it must be retained.[2] He says sexual relations must be indulged in as a kind of *yagna*, wherein the semen must be retained. That according to him is true *Brahamacharya*. Many ancient teachers have expounded on the intimate connection between blood and semen, a theory that is perhaps linked to male anxieties regarding their libido, penis size and the belief that ejaculating leads to loss of energy. Ayurveda attributes the generation of a single drop of semen to approximately eighty drops of blood. Warning one to keep off the sexual radar, everyday analogies are used to drive home the point saying that just as buttermilk is thinned when one skims off the butter, semen too is thinned by its spilling, the more the wastage, more is the weakening of its essential *tattwa* – its energizing power. In the Yoga Shastras it is said: *Maranam bindupatanat jivanam bindu-rakshanat*. Falling of semen brings death; preservation of semen gives life. A similar sentiment finds expression in the letters that so many men write to sexologists in magazines, various portals and agony aunt columns, where they speak about their fear at the prospect of losing their masculine vigour, because of masturbation and the loss of seminal fluid. Travelling through the small towns of India or even the suburbs of large cities, one comes across a plethora of such advertisements – in giant lettering on public walls, messages on the backs of auto rickshaws, posters stuck on lamp posts, offering the ultimate solution for the troubled soul worrying about the loss of libido.

When talking of celibacy, it's a rare guru like Swami Sivananda who makes no distinction between women and men on the path to salvation. He was a visionary who opened the spiritual world for several women and men. 'Women too must follow this spiritual path and keep away from the sexual path, even though their physiognomies are different,' he writes. In both cases there is a depletion of vital fluids, which is an obstacle in neutralizing the raging demands of the body, a vital need in the pursuit of the spiritual. Endorsing this view mythology upholds the example of Hanuman, the bachelor God. His devotion to Lord Rama is legendary, and his magnificent strength is directly attributed to the *tapas* of his *brahmacharya*. In the Mahabharata, Bhishma was blessed with *ichcha mrityu* – he could choose the moment of his own death – a boon granted to him for his oath of eternal celibacy.

Celibacy is prescribed in other religions as well.[3] In the Christian orders for instance, virgins and celibates were the earliest communities to achieve positions of prominence. The Virgin mother's holiness and divinity are qualified by her name. In the Roman Catholic church, only unmarried men and women were permitted to become priests and nuns, and in early Greek treatises, celibacy was seen as necessary to attain higher knowledge. Plato believed that it was necessary to suppress bodily desires so that the soul can be free to search for knowledge. Plotinus the Greek philosopher too endorsed this view.

That sex depletes energy and vitality, is a belief that has taken root amongst many sports persons as well. Their theory is that sexual activity before a match can lead to a bad performance. Coaches often flash 'red cards' at their players in the ticking hours before the matches, preventing them and sometimes banning them from sex.[4,5] Though all manners of studies and tests have been conducted, nothing definite has been discovered to prove such theories.[6] Some psychologists though have rather hesitantly forwarded the theory, that the reason behind all those curfew hours, is because fulfilling sex creates a kind of torpor that blunts the killer instinct. The sports world being notoriously superstitious, has perhaps built some strategies around such nebulous theories, hoping for great performances by keeping their players hungry and raring to go.

Women: A Spiritual Quest

Patriarchy though gives little space to a woman's independent quest for spiritual knowledge. Instead, it invokes the traditional duties of women as their path to salvation. Manusmriti states that a woman's spiritual life is confined to her role as a householder, where the worship of her husband is her scriptural path. This effectively bars her from seeking spiritual salvation independently. There is a twisted rationale behind this injunction: 'Renunciation of marriage and family ties for a life of celibacy, asceticism, and spiritual discipline is one of the most provocative options that can be chosen by a woman.' In choosing to live an independent life, where she rejects 'belonging' to a man, a woman effectively says no to her traditional roles of wife and mother. Instead, she aspires for the male privilege of being either a householder or an ascetic. As Catherine Ojha puts it, 'The male ascetic is a man who has made a choice between the ideals in life equally allowed for him. But the female ascetic is a woman who, having renounced the single mode of life set for her, adopts a behaviour primarily intended for males.'[7]

Scholars have pointed out that female celibacy and renunciation involves two parallel stories. One, women's role of perpetuating the family by bearing children and taking care of the family and home, leaving the man free to follow his choices, is directly upended by her rejection of sex, and thereby family life. And two, a woman's choice over her sexuality challenges the fundamental patriarchal impulse to control women.[8,9,10]

Given the wildly opposing viewpoints offered by different ascetics, Indian women have chosen one of two options to embark on their spiritual journeys. Some of the female saints were married, such as Anasuya Devi (1923–1985) or Sharda Ma, consort of Ramakrishna Paramhansa; suggesting perhaps that the householder's duties can embrace the ascetic as well.[11] Interestingly, within the confines of marriage, many women shun sexual relations, seeing in this abstinence the path to attain spiritual enlightenment. These women are both vehicles for the Goddess and thus subject to Her command, while also enjoying status, influence, and control within their families and devotees who solicit the Goddess' favour through them. Numerous biographies and accounts of Ramakrishna Paramhansa's life talk about his relationship with Sharda ma, as that of a son with his mother. There are other spiritual gurus too who have rejected the householder's life, such as Anandmurti Gurumaa; Ma Amritanandmayee, and many others. Though these female gurus were subjected to tremendous pressures to adopt the householder's life, they not only embraced the life of the renunciate, but opened the possibilities of their women disciples to follow religious practices that they were traditionally barred from, like the recitation of Sanskrit mantras, the celebration of the Upanayana or the thread ceremony etc.

Jainism too offers a well-defined path for ascetic women. Today, Jain sadhvis or nuns outnumber the monks in a four to one ratio giving rise to the conjecture that a disproportionately large number of women were becoming nuns because renunciation provided them a refuge from the ignominy of a widow's life. Many modern-day scholars however debunk this theory considering it a great disservice to the spirit of *vairagya* or dissociation from the worldly, that these women bring to their spiritual pursuit. A more nuanced study shows instead that many women become nuns to escape patriarchal structures and the restricted roles it reserves for householders.[12] In that sense they reject patriarchy, making sadhvis the only 'free and individuated women' within the context of Indic religions, even earning respect and recognition.

Often those who are dedicated to public causes and are single in this country, are called 'dedicated crusaders'. Single women in particular are additionally endowed with wonderful sobriquets that invoke a host of female relatives. Jayalalitha, who ruled Tamil Nadu like a colossus for much of her political life, was respectfully called Amma, Mamata Banerjee the current chief minister of West Bengal is addressed as a wise and caring didi, Mayavati the founder of the Bahujan Samaj Party is behen ji, while Sonia Gandhi, is the venerable matriarchal figure in the Congress party. The Prime Minister Narendra Modi is projected as a single man, though that is not entirely true since in his electoral nomination papers he had declared his marriage. And Rahul Gandhi, who was the president of the Congress Party during the 2019 general elections, remains an eligible single man; his single status provoking periodic bouts of curiosity in the media and the public.

Popular Art and the Single Woman

When it comes to portraying single women, popular cinema and literature follow a well-worn path. If she's young, she is portrayed as nubile and often objectified. The focus of the male gaze, her beauty is dissected and hyperbolic analogies used to describe the effect of her attractiveness on men. She is the muse of music, poetry and art, the inspiration behind perennially popular songs like: *Chaudhvi ka chaand ho ya aftaab ho* ... your beauty is like the moon in its fullness or like the sun? In a later avatar we have songs such as this one from the movie Ai Dil Hai Mushkil, where there is a shift from the ethereal poetry of earlier songs to a more nuanced but contemporary expression of what the loved one means to the singer: *Tu safar hai mera, tu hi meri manzil.. tu mera khuda, tu hi dua mein hai shamil, tere bina guzara, ai dil hai mushkil.* You are my journey, and my destination. The object of my worship, you are in my prayers..to live in your absence, o my heart is so difficult.

An older woman mostly shown as single, has traditionally had her character written along fairly predictable lines. Often she is a figure of dependency, where she is a part of the supporting cast as the aunt or widowed mother, but never the agent herself. Her character is painted in binaries, either as cloyingly sweet and sacrificing or as the conniving manipulator, jealous of other people's completeness. In a survey [13] by Gransnet and HQ of more than 1,000 women over 40, it has found that more than half (51%) feel that older women in books do fall into "cliched roles". Fifty per cent of the women surveyed said that older characters are shown "as baffled by smartphones, computers or the internet." In another book: *Ageing Women in Literature and Visual Culture,*[14] the author, traces the history of the depiction of women in the popular arts in the early European period, as stereotypical images affected by the prevalent cultural viewpoints. Older women were typically shown as witches, crones or hags; in art the older woman was shown as the lower class servant, whose 'weather-beaten, desiccated body was in contrast to the beautiful, ivory-skinned young lady (the focus of the painting). Indian paintings in the times of Raja Ravi Verma, too subscribed to the image of a woman as comely and young, of statuesque, Ajantaesque proportions, though modern narratives in the works of painters like Vaikuntham, Paresh Maity Bharti Kher, have moved away from this image of apsara -like beauty to showing the inner landscape. The early painter (in India) who worked on the female body and wrested it away from the male gaze was perhaps Amrita Sher Gill, whose nudes did not represent the typical erotic sensuality that normally nudes were shown as, but directed the gaze to the inner being. In the entertainment business, Madonna the pop icon, has of late been garnering press, whose focus has shifted unforgivably to her 'age', rather than her mind-boggling talent or music performances, with her song not included in the BBC playlist as she was considered too old![15] In the television show *Good morning Britain*, Piers Morgan pretended to vomit as he saw her dancing, claiming 'I loved Madonna when she acted her age[..] you can't be 58 and be prancing about.' To which Madonna's own rejoinder as she accepted the 'Billboard's Women of the Year' award was that she had been inspired by David Bowie who played by no rules. But as a woman she realized that for a woman there were always rules. 'You are allowed to be pretty cute, sexy .. objectified but do not age, to age is to sin, you will be criticized, vilified and will not be played on the radio.'[16]

There is Tagore's character of the widow Binodini in his book, *Chokher Bali*, made into a movie in 2000, where Tagore explores the psychology of a youngish single woman, marginalized by social strictures because of her widowhood, and who over time becomes an insidiously jealous presence in the lives of her relatives. There are of course hundreds of mother-in-law figures often widowed, who are depicted in movies as being scheming and wicked such as in the movie 'Beta' an Anil Kapoor and Madhuri Dixit starrer, where the mother played by Aruna Irani has a typically stereotypical role, where she is shown constantly plotting against her step-son. The type-casting doesnot flag, as gender prejudices and ageing remain a volatile combination for women. The Khan trio now all nudging their 50's continue to cavort with ever younger heroines while their contemporaries like Madhuri Dixit are already being pushed into roles dripping gravitas. But there's hope yet .

New treatments, new ways of looking at older women characters, many of them single are changing viewers perceptions. Look at Aishwarya Rai playing the character of Saba Taliyarkhan in the movie Ai Dil Hai Mushkil, where she is single, older,, gives off the whiff of her own wealth, is shown making love to Ayan played by Ranbir Kapoor, a younger man, and then leaves him on her own terms with a dialogue that endorses her fierce independence: main *kisiki zaroorat nahin khwaish banana chahti hoon*. I will not accept being just a crutch but want to someone's aspiration.

In Hollywood the newfound public awareness of sexism and gender inequality along with the #MeToo movement, has certainly set off a trend for making movies that are stepping beyond the usual practice of featuring the woman as a sexy, young addon to the hero's towering presence. Instead older woman are being given new experimental roles, such as director.[17] Claire Denis' new romantic dramedy *Let the Sunshine In*, where the award-winning Juliette Binoche plays Isabelle, a middle aged woman who isn't offering a Hollywood portrayal of a middle-aged woman, but uses her sexuality freely in her role as a Parisian artist.

The signs are all around us. Prominent women in the west, who have routinely faced the sexist eye and been hounded for tipping over the 'age limit' are now unabashedly proclaiming their age and asserting their right to be in the public eye, as encompassed in this headline: 'I am an (older) woman hear me roar!'[18] Agatha Christie's famous character, the original path breaker Miss Marple, an intelligent single woman, living life on her own terms, seems to be becoming more of a role model than she ever was.[19]

Continuing the exploration of women's lives as shaped by external forces, we find that the two major influences on Indian psyche regarding women's spaces have been the Manusmriti and Bharata's Natya Shastra.[20] The former is focuses on morality and was meant to counter the aggressive spread of Buddhism and Jainism. As Wendy Doniger, an American Indologist and religious scholar says, Manusmriti 'was pivotal in the priestly response to the crisis of traditional Aryan culture.' The British adopted it as a personal law during the colonial period, giving it a semi-legal legitimacy that soon became the last word on the laws dictating the Hindu way of life including the woman's role and conduct. The British took the lazy way out, resorting to Manu as the ultimate authority on Hinduism's complexities, in their attempt to navigate the labyrinth of codes and strictures regarding Hindu caste and religious practices. Manu's code professed a limited engagement for women outside of the domestic sphere. In some of his pronouncements he is an outright misogynist. Contrarily though, he also tries to redeem his earlier bias with a statement such as this, here Manu says: Where women are revered, there the gods rejoice; but where they are not, no rite bears fruit.[21]

From the religious we come to the other end of the spectrum - the *nayika*, the heroine as depicted in the *Natya Shastra*. This work laid emphasis on the performing arts such as dance, music and theatre, and was in many ways a compendium on how the human body can use different mudras or gestures to convey a range of complex emotions. Though patriarchy ensured that women from normal households confined their desire for singing and dancing only within women designated spaces, whereas female performers catered almost exclusively to men. None of the strictures of purity and chastity extended to them. Conversely this allowed them economic freedom and an agency that the woman of 'virtue' suffocating behind their all-enveloping purdah, could have hardly imagined.

But there was a price to pay for such seemingly libertine values. Many were pushed into the roles of the courtesan, and were labelled morally loose and 'available'. Even in modern times, endless stories abound about women in the nayika role. The famous Akhtari Bai or Begum Akhtar, whose early life of exploitation has been extensively chronicled even as she surged towards fame, only gained respectability by marrying a highly-regarded man, and becoming a doyen of Hindustani classical music.[22] Others were star attractions in their chosen fields, though the unforgiving social gaze left them vulnerable to the exploitations of the men in their lives, who could be their agents, lovers, patrons and even husbands. Singers Gauhar Bai and Jaddan Bai, the theatre actor Binodini Dasi are some of those famous names, whose personal lives were riven by the schizophrenia of social morality of their times.

Despite fame, money and the satisfaction of fulfilling their creative expression, the hypocritical society compelled these women artistes to feel that their lives were inferior to the purdah-clad women shuttered behind their respectable doors, whose ironically claustrophobic lives have been hauntingly depicted in the literature of Ashapurna Devi the famous Bengali author, the Gyan Peeth awardee Indira Goswami, and Bimal Mitra, the writer of such famous works as *Sahib, Bibi aur Ghulam*, which was later made into a movie by Guru Dutt. Like male artistes they too yearned to inhabit the twin world of artistic creativity and the respectability of family life, but patriarchy would not forgive these nayikas for answering their creative calling outside of their stifling domestic roles, and punished them by withholding the privilege of family life from these 'fallen women'. Shunned from respectable society, with the pejorative labels of *baijis* and *tawaif*, these women were reduced to looking at their single status with despair and deep-rooted guilt, in sharp contrast to today, where an artiste would take justifiable pride in her achievements without despairing over being single.

Different Kinds of Alliances

Nearly a century later, as various studies have shown, marriage continues to have primacy in the country's socio-cultural milieu. Yet there are significant changes. As a society in transition, various kinds of realities seem to coexist, despite the overwhelming percentage of the population opting for marriage. There are those who have rejected marriage, or explored other ways of finding companionship such as live-in relationships. There are same-sex couples who are technically single as their marriage is yet to be recognized in India, There are also those who got married, and then for whatever reason opted for separation or divorce, and some who have lost their partners. People are also delaying marriage, as career aspirations have pushed it to the backseat.

To connect language and perceptions, it's interesting to find that Indian languages like Hindi for instance, do not employ the pejorative terminology of the Chinese, who have terms like '*shenghu*', or leftovers, for women who remain unmarried by the age of 27. Nor is there an equivalent of the English term 'spinster', which suggests Victorian images of a crusty aunt beyond her prime marriageable years. Sociologist E. Kay Trimberger in her article 'Single Women in India: Rarer, Riskier, and Happier Than in the U.S.' alludes to this unique aspect of the Hindu worldview, where the single woman is not necessarily deemed unattractive or unhappy.[23] Indian languages of course have references to the word *kanya*, which is imbued with the positive imagery of a young girl or woman who has some agency. Feminists in India elaborate on the positive image of a single woman within the Indian social fabric: 'We are still heavily steeped in the old Indian tradition which holds that voluntary sexual abstinence bestows extraordinary power on human beings ... Our culture has the remarkable ability to provide special space and respect for women who voluntarily opt out of the sexual, marital role.'[24] And yet the single woman is seen as someone peculiar, by choice or circumstance.

According to the Census of 2011, India's single woman population is poised at 73 million and growing. 21 per cent of the country's 353 million women above the age of 20 are single – a rise of nearly 40 per cent since the 2001 census. The 20-29 age group has shown the sharpest rise, which at nearly 68 per cent tells us a story that India needs to recognize and create space for. It raises some urgent questions whose answers will give direction to the surging ambitions and aspirations of millions of women, who are shaping an India that is radically different from the one they were born in. The reality lies somewhere on the spectrum between the reviled and the revered, since singledom is not a homogenous state but has important intersections with gender, culture and religion.

The gaze directed at the single woman is dictated by her age. As a kanya, very young and virginal, she is revered as the manifestation of the Goddess in her various avatars. But beyond a certain age, the single woman provokes a different gaze, which has to be contextualized against the existing social fabric. Whether unmarried, divorced, widowed, or those who don't identify with binary heterosexual classifications, she attracts a different set of challenges than those faced by the single woman in the developed world. A woman who isn't married by a certain age is seen as a family's failing, a challenge to the institution of marriage, and to patriarchy's predetermined role for her. The division of household labour is no longer applicable to her, nor is her sexuality harnessed within the parameters of a wife and all that it entails. A traditional society like India therefore still finds it difficult to deal with a woman who has not been married by a certain age. Hence, she is subjected to constant 'frank' interrogations by society at large. 'Why are you not married?' remains everyone's concern as if it were civic duty.[25]

Even supportive parents, find the external pressure difficult to take. This includes even those women who haven't rejected marriage but have merely put it on hold, face interrogation. Though 'marriageable age' is purely notional, yet it hangs like a highway sign over the young. In a BBC article that evoked a lot of responses, a young woman wrote, 'At 28, ideally I would have been married for a couple of years. By Indian standards, I've left it late and I am probably at the bottom of the pyramid of eligible women. But I still don't find the idea of "settling for" someone appealing.'[26] Men are not entirely exempt from these pressures, though it might be delayed for them. In response to the above article, Pratik says, 'For my family, 28, would be the limit to get married, I would not get decent girls and my value in the "market" will go down. I resent this.'[27]

Survey Points to Changing Attitudes

But women are increasingly pushing the envelope far beyond their twenties, as jobs in a market economy demand commitment and focus. My NGO, Women Work & Health Initiative (WWHI) conducted a survey in March 2019 amongst 25 women and men, ages 20-30 years, residing in Bengaluru, Kolkata and Delhi. The idea was to understand attitudes to marriage. Only one of the respondents was married while the rest were delaying the process, standing rock solid against parental diktats, particularly the girls. The need to adjust to the husband's household remains a given for the woman, but the expectation certainly takes its toll, leading to more divorces in its wake. For men, career concerns are a big reason for delaying marriage, and at least a couple of them admitted that they wished to savour their freedom for a while longer, before getting into the 'headache' of managing a wife and children.

Rana Dasgupta, in his book *Capital*, talks about these rising anxieties amongst Indian men.[28] He traces its origins as far back as the colonial period, when men had to learn to live within a world of do's and don'ts as laid out by their colonisers. This would sometimes entail a suppressing of the soul as the humiliations of enslavement were heaped on them. The women by contrast, confined to their home, became by default the keepers of the spiritual and moral order in that space, where the man could still come back at the end of the day and be treated as king. Now that many women from the middle-classes have stepped out of that sanctified space, and are battling the daily challenges of work and career, the gender equations have shifted. The men, uncomprehending and angry at this change, release their frustrations on the women whose independence directly challenges their own growing irrelevance.

A positive side effect of women's financial independence is that marrying for money is no longer the raging rationale for rushing into matrimony.[29] As Sushmita Sen, the former Miss Universe and Bollywood actor, puts it in her own inimitable style: 'I don't need a man in my life to have diamonds. I can own them myself.' While this maybe her way of shutting up the media inquiring about the man who had gifted her an outsized diamond weighing down her pretty finger, the logic applies equally to those who lay no claim to movie-star status. Working women are earning well and investing in assets, just like their male counterparts. In the WWHI survey, when asked about what exactly were they looking for in a marriage, most respondents, both women and men, ticked – love, companionship, status and sex partners as their choices. Financial security featured only for a couple of women.

The ticking biological clock is less threatening too, as modern medicine makes it possible to have babies beyond the 'crossover' age. The trend has certainly caught in India, as reflected in the market for Assisted Reproductive Technologies, which is an approximately $5 billion a year and growing steadily. IVF clinics have mushroomed everywhere and surrogate wombs were available in plenty until recently, till the government got into the act and has introduced a bill that bans it.[30,31]

And What of the Men?

How is this changing scenario, triggered by education, economics and medical science, affecting relations between men and women? For one the man's role within the cocoon of marriage is changing. The entitlement and power guaranteed to the male as the provider is under some stress, as women's roles too are becoming equally, if not more, challenging. In certain homes there is also a fluidity of roles as men become more participative in the upbringing of the children. But this upending of the patriarchal status quo is resulting in palpable tension in some cases, with attempts to push back to the old ways. Scorched marriages are becoming more common, making young people very cautious before tying the knot. Especially women, who still have the onus of embracing a new family and culture.

We now know that it is not only single women who have to fend off the overwhelming shaadi ka pressure, but also men. These pressures have very real consequences, and while its impact on women is often discussed, few people talk about the subversive effect this has on men's lives, as they look for careers where they can out earn their future wives. 'The reality is that Indian society's attitude towards marriage, places huge constraints on the life choices of males as well. Yes, a man can wait until his late 20s and early 30s before seriously looking for a life partner without having to worry about finding a desirable mate. Unlike women, a man does not have to choose between a career and a family. But the pressure of earning a higher income than his partner in order to provide for his family limits the professional choices of men.'[32]

Once their adult son is established in a 'safe' profession, parents start working on the next stage of 'settling' him by scouting for a suitable girl. In the traditional world of arranged marriages, this is when parents with daughters of 'marriageable age' begin to make anxious enquires and try to take the match forward. Finally, the man after some dithering takes the inescapable path to marriage and 'settles down'. The script is inherently lop-sided where the girl's parents behave almost like supplicants, creating a situation rife for the enactment of the power play that reveals itself in all its stark inequality during the wedding. Though if the girl is well educated and has a good job, the power dynamics work differently.

Some men may resist this pressure to fall in line, but they are considered oddities in a marriage-oriented society. Parents are known to take up vows and prayers, much like the mothers of unmarried daughters, for divine intervention to get their sons to agree to marriage.

Divorce: The Other Side of the Coin

The conflict between traditions moored in time and the expectations of young people in a changing society, is being reflected in the growing divorce rates and separations. Once considered an urban reality, it has moved into provincial towns as well. Mumbai which has the highest divorce rate in the country, had in 11,667 cases of divorce in 2014 as compared to 5245 in 2010. In Kolkata, there has been a 350 per cent increase from 2,388 cases in 2003 to 8,347 in 2014. And yet these figures seem to flag a mere 1.1 per cent of the nation's marriages heading for the courts, a miniscule nothingness when compared with USA's 50 per cent divorces.[33]

So, does this mean that Indian couples complete the seven pheras and live in heavenly bliss ever afterwards? As always, the story is couched in sub-plots. Ruth Vanita, feminist and gay scholar points out that in a country where most marriages remain unregistered, it would be farfetched to imagine that couples would approach the courts for divorce.[34] Besides, many women and men live separately without going through the process of divorce. The sense of *izzat* or family honour and 'what people will say' too keep disgruntled emotions tamped down, and couples play their roles for the outside world. Activists like Prof. Vibhuti Patel heading the Women's Studies Centre at TISS, Mumbai point out that in a country where a majority of the women still do not have an independent income nor the agency to make decisions, it is really difficult for them to end a marriage, unless it's something that is quite unbearable. Where do they go, who will support them, are the big questions that they have to answer before taking the next step. And though social conditions are changing, women find it tough after a divorce.

A *New York Times* blog has a different story to tell, where a seasoned divorce lawyer in Delhi says that one reason that people stay away from divorce is because of the difficult process of litigation, which requires repeated visits to the courts, which is both emotionally traumatic and a drain on one's resources.[35] Since there has been no national census done on divorce in India, we can only rely on some surveys. The Economic Research Foundation of India surveyed a random selection of some 405 urban and rural Indian women. It seems that one of the reasons for increasing divorce rates is a huge mismatch between traditional expectations and modern-day aspirations. The modern looking but traditional thinking woman, conforming to the old-fashioned template of a dutiful daughter-in-law as played out in soap operas, still seems to influence prospective in-laws. I had once attended a family court in the town of Jhansi, where a couple was on the verge of separation because of in-law issues, the major complaint being that the woman ate her breakfast before her in-laws and husband, thereby disrupting the hierarchical order. Even though she was up at the crack of dawn to do the household chores!

On the other side, young working women who value their independence, still cling to traditional notions of what their in-laws owe them as financial and social support. When that is wanting, frustration and anger sets in. Incompatibility, differing personalities, outlooks and interests, are all emerging as major reasons for couples deciding to split.

But what is life like after a divorce? This question was posed in separate conversations with some twenty people in their twenties and thirties, who were separated or divorced recently. Seventy-five per cent of the respondents were women, everyone came from a middle-class background, though there were substantial variations in their incomes, ranging from ₹25,000 to ₹1,00,000 a month or more. They came from both provincial and metro cities. After they split up, did they feel lonely, angry, socially marginalized and guilty? The answers had a certain similarity. Neeta, thirty years old, went for a mutually agreed divorce after five years of marriage. She wanted out because she found the parents-in-law overbearing even though they lived in another town, her husband too malleable, and despite having a child, she thought she had had enough. Salil her husband, had a different point of view. He was attached to his parents, but since they were not living together, he really couldn't understand why his parents were an issue. He says that he was willing to compromise and wanted her to come back, but their on-again, off-again attempts at reconciling soon reached a dead end. And so, they went to the courts, as the only solution.

A common response that has changed from previous generations is that divorcees, no longer wrap themselves in the terrible shame and guilt like in previous generations. Rati, now in her late forties, is settled in Indore as a senior school teacher and is doing well for herself. She got divorced in 1997 five years after her marriage. 'It was tough to survive in the early years after I had left him, Anil,' she adds consciously reminding herself of his name. 'He was a drunkard, used to beat me up. I had no money as I was not working, and I had to be very strong to leave him and come back to my parents with my two children. Initially, I felt the shame of everyone's stares. Even the school teachers where I took up a job, would ask, so where is your husband, why did you leave him? They used to get a perverse kind of pleasure in this question. I felt a kind of shame all the time.' Today, she smiles at her decision seeing that her battle has worked out well for her and her children, and she has made a leap forward on the aspirational ladder.

And if one thinks about it deeply, this is a welcome change for our society. To quote writer Amit Varma, 'Rising divorce rates tell us one thing for sure: that more and more women are finding the means, and the independence, to walk out of bad marriages and live life on their own terms. If we judge ourselves as a society on the state of our women – and surely that must be a parameter – then this is good news. We do not need to credit either feminism or Western culture for this – the emancipation of women in real terms, across the world, has been enabled by technology, and can be explained most easily with economics.'[36]

Divorce is not always because of violence or dowry. Increasingly, as couples are coping with the push and pull of juggling work, raising kids, running a house, peer pressure, their own egos and chemistry, and often without the cushioned support of a joint family, marriage ends up bearing the brunt of it all. And unlike earlier, the divorced woman doesn't always go back to her parents, but is exploring new options of leading an independent life away from the parental fold.

The lifestyle changes after a divorce affect both women and men in very similar ways. Niraj, a 32-year-old employee in an MNC, who was divorced recently, shares that though the divorce has brought relief from the constant fights, he feels odd going for couple dinners with his friends. And the emptiness of the house in the mornings and the nights, they are the worst. 'Sex, that too is a big problem,' he admits, 'how much can one chat up the girls, you tell me?' For women, access to sex is even more difficult. Brinda, 35 years old, finally opted for a divorce after being married for ten years. With two daughters, she has moved back to Kanpur to live with her aunt. She talks about the extreme loneliness she faces at times, as life has cast her into sacrosanct roles of a mother, niece, teacher at the local school. 'But where is the romance in my life?' she asks. 'And sex, I have almost forgotten that there is a part of my body that gave me pleasure.' She uses the Hindi term for orgasm, 'sukh'. 'But now,' she says almost conspiratorially, 'my friends have told me I can go on my phone to sex sites and watch all that,' and she adds, 'maybe I can join other couples, you know for sex, my friend tells me lots of people are doing it.'

Brinda is not alone in looking at other possibilities for satisfying the physical senses. According to a survey conducted by *India Today*, a female respondent said, 'Like 1 in 7 of my fellow urban citizens, who sleep with people whose names they do not know, I believe in exploring the full dynamism of that elusive human experience called sex. On the surface, we appear normal. But how we feel on the inside is a different story: indistinguishable from the happily smug men and women in the midst of India's new plenty, we inhabit hidden depths across the country. How well does the nation know us?'[37]

The World of the LGBTQIA+

Increasingly, the LGBTQIA+ community has been openly rejecting the heteronormative definition of a relationship or marriage in India. The latest census informs us that the transgender community comprises of some 4,90,000 individuals, though activists estimate the actual figures to be six or seven times that number.

In 2012, when the draconian Section 377 of the Indian Penal Code was still in force, NACO (National Aids Control Society) estimated the gay population to be about 25 million. Queer activists like Ashok Row Kavi, however put the figures realistically at 50 million. Activists pointed out that other queer identities had not been added to the figure, and NACO had merely focussed on its own target group which were MSMs (men who have sex with men).[38]

Though Section 377 has been repealed and homosexuality has been legally decriminalized, sexuality and identity in general remains deeply suppressed and undiscussed in Indian society. As Upasana, co-founder of Amra Odbhut Café, a beautiful space for queer individuals says, 'Given what society is like, few women have the options of exploring their sexuality, or acknowledging or even knowing that they don't wish to share a bed or exchange wedding vows with a man. Men though are much surer of identity, given the spaces to cruise and find partners, or pose sexily on gay sites. But no one is interested in getting married. They had rather have a beautiful relationship with their partner. Gay marriages remain a privileged, Western concept, which does not touch the realities of Indian life, where more pressing issues of discrimination are subverted by this glamorous depiction ... Is there such a thing as the traditional marriage? Today you have these open marriages, where couples have an understanding about having open sexual relationships, some people have multiple encounters, there are gay men who marry a woman to hide it from society; sometimes even the other way around. Who is to judge what is right?'

Homophobia most likely came to India during the colonial period, when British missionaries and educationists attacked liberal Indian attitudes towards same-sex relationships, *kinnars* and eunuchs, with Macaulay finally deciding to rein in the native's freewheeling ways with his infamous law in 1861 prohibiting 'carnal intercourse against the order of nature with any man, woman or animal'. A law that criminalized intimate and consensual acts of love for more than 150 years, until it was finally scrapped in 2018. This was a law that was inspired by an even more primitive model – the sixteenth century English law called the Buggery Law introduced under the reign of Henry VIII, which India was zealously upholding until 2018.[39,40]

For centuries before colonization, Indian art, literature and mythology have had an easy relationship with different sexual identities. As historians and gay-rights activists have shared, a broad spectrum of gender and sexual identities and activities have been represented and discussed in Indian literature for two millennia in non-judgemental and even celebratory ways. This is illustrated through sculptures in the temples of Khajuraho and Konark, yogini temples, and in tantric illustrations, where same-sex love has been graphically depicted, besides the explicit sculptures of various sexual acts. But the Indian upper class, desperate to appease their prudish colonial masters, tried to erase all kinds of allusions to homosexuality in their literature. Instead they brought in an aggressive form of heterosexuality into their discourse as a form of hyper masculinity, which they felt the English would better appreciate. This erasure was so indiscriminate and obtrusive that even the Urdu ghazal, which gendered both lover and beloved as male, often metaphorically referring to God and his believer, was not spared this sanitizing process.

Within Hinduism itself, there are varying opinions regarding homosexuality. Some like Baba Ramdev condemn it unequivocally as a disorder, which can be 'cured' through proper treatment.[41] On the other hand, the revered philosopher Jiddu Krishnamurti when asked about his views on homosexuality said, 'This has been a question for thousands and thousands and thousands of years. It isn't something new ... These are facts. Right? As heterosexuality is a fact. Homosexuality exists in the world, in different parts of the world very common, other parts of the world it is practically unknown ... Why do we make it such an enormous problem?'[42] He asks almost rhetorically suggesting as it were, that different forms of sexuality coexist, and one cannot say this or that is right or wrong, for there can be no absolutes. Ruth Vanita points out that in the Hindu narrative, there is a recurring theme where authority figures who oppose an individual's passionate love are compelled to give in when they realize that their love is irresistible. As the eleventh-century Kathasaritsagara story-cycle states in the context of an intense male-male attraction at first sight: '*Vakti janmaantarapritim manah snihyadakaaranam*'. Affection that arises in the heart without a cause speaks of love persisting from a former birth.

Stephen Fry's documentary *Out There*, which looks at the oppression of gay people around the world, has a telling and rather touching scene where he is talking to the parents of a gay man in south India. To all appearances a rather traditional Brahmin family, with the caste marks on the forehead proclaiming their status, one would expect stringent condemnation of their son's 'aberrant' choice. But the older couple surprise everyone by accepting their son's sexual preference and welcoming his partner too. But not everyone is as accepting and willing to educate themselves about 'others'. Different thought processes are at work when dealing with the complex subject of non-normative sexualities. Though homosexuality isn't legally criminal any more, yet its complete social and cultural acceptance has a long, long way to go.

Many parents really don't care what the courts decide about homosexuality; 'our kid must get married the right way', they insist. In this ignorant denial, many pressurize their gay children into getting married, causing untold misery and heartbreak, often forcing them to keep their sexual orientation under wraps. Many fail to understand why their son, since in most cases the men admit more openly to their sexual orientation, cannot have a 'regular' marriage. Sudhir Kakar in his book *The Indians*, alludes to this dismissive attitude of parents towards queer sensibilities, their sole purpose being to gain the fig leaf of marriage.[43] Eligible gay men are harangued with proposals until they run out of excuses about why they cannot accept them. Soon these turn into rumours about impotency and orientation. Even when the answers are staring them in the face, parents think that queerness is a passing phase and is curable through a host of remedies such as charms, yoga, mystical healers, charlatans and the biggest cure of them all – marriage to a woman.

Vijay (name changed), a 34-year-old working as the customer interface of an automobile showroom in a small town in Haryana, talks about his marriage some ten years ago. It's difficult to get him to open up, but after a while he begins his story, 'I didn't want to get married, I had told my elder sister and her husband, who was manager in a big private company. He even got me a job there for a while. I kept saying no to didi, but she didn't listen to me, they thought I was feeling sad about mummy's recent death. Even at the *baraat* I kept saying no, but no one heard me. I dreaded the wedding night. I didn't want to touch her. I am not interested in that sort of thing, never have been. I had told that to didi, but they said it will be okay, once you get married. Things became very bad with my wife, she called me names, kept asking why I had spoilt her life, didn't tell her that I am not interested in women. After sometime her father came and took her away.' In arranged marriages, a girl's assumed virginity is a critical parameter for acceptance. A failed first marriage, hardly promotes her bid for a second, notwithstanding the skewed cards dealt to her.

'It's an exercise in delusion, with the parents and the son all guilty of misleading a woman,' says a gay activist. And the consequences can be calamitous for everyone involved. Priya Vedi, a doctor 'put an end to her life claiming that she could not bear the torture inflicted by her gay husband'. Their marriage had remained unconsummated, and though she learnt of his orientation six months after their marriage, she hoped that she would be able to turn him around.[44] Unfortunately, this is not an isolated incident, with many gay men using marriage as a camouflage and when the opportunity presents itself, many begin to cruise for partners through the safety of the internet. Ashok Row Kavi, a prominent LGBT rights activist reveals just such a story: One of the most common problems I've faced as a community counsellor is of married gay men and their issues. I still remember a young married man who wished to know how to "balance" his life with a wife at home and a male lover in the army, of all things. Talking about gay marriage he has obviously had a rethink, though he is against marriage, he wants the Supreme Court to confer marriage rights to gay people because he has learnt that 'Marriage confers on people certain rights and entitlements by the State that cannot be imagined away.'[45,46]

The Solo Life

Singlehood is rising across societies and yet there are not enough studies to explain its causes and consequences. Dr Jill Reynolds in her book, *The Single Woman: A Discursive Investigation*, explores singleness from several perspectives, her research aided by her interviews with some thirty women in the UK between the ages of 30–60. Her aim was to understand how women deal with singleness. She looks at the theories of several social scientists who see singleness amongst women from two different lens. In one view she is empowered. Economic and sexual liberation have made her strong and she is no longer beholden to a man. While others see the single woman as a threat to traditional society, which is affecting family life and community. Other than being caught in a bind, Reynolds's book also points out that single women go through relationships which are coloured by a patriarchal view, where the ideal is still the man-woman one.[47] Though many women are happy being single, the societal expectation, unmasked even in the developed world, doesn't escape them. Even if they don't intend to marry, but the pressure to be in a romantic relationship is ever-present. They feel they have failed somewhere, as long-term relationships are seen as a marker of success in life.

As sociologist Eric Klinenberg mentions in his widely popular book, *Going Solo, The Extraordinary Rise and Surprising Appeal of Going Alone*, there are more single people today than ever before. 'The rise in living alone is the biggest modern social change that we have yet to name or identify,' is the tag-line in his talks. Klinenberg traces the history of singleness in America from the 1940s when loneliness and even immorality, was associated with it. Today with 31 million single people comprising 28 per cent of households in the US, America like other parts of Europe, is witnessing a singles' revolution. This is not only about the middle-aged or the old, but increasingly the 30-plus age group is making it their choice. He attributes it to several factors such as affluence, the rising status of women and their greater autonomy, the communication revolution, specially the internet and social media, the rise of modern cities, and the last – that an ageing population wants to live alone because that gives them dignity and integrity.[48]

India too is seeing a huge rise in the numbers of its single population. Single women reportedly constitute 21 per cent of India's female population, which is close to 73 million in number (Census 2011).[49] Singlehood of course is not a hegemonic state and includes the state of divorced, separated, widowed and unmarried women. What are the choices open to them and how are they viewed in society are questions that will need urgent attention. Different authors and journalists have shed light on these in their own unique way. Sreemoyee Piu Kundu in an article headlined: 'Is Single the New Black? For Indian Women, it's Complicated,' through interviews with various women, seems to say that the going is indeed tough in the country. According to her, single women confess 'to a gnawing sense of loneliness, the looming anxiety about the onset of old age, health issues, of losing parents, siblings and friends over time, of personal security, of being elderly and alone.'[50]

A major discriminatory practice singles face is finding a place to rent. Eminent journalist Namita Bhandare[51] interviews Shikha Makan, a film-maker about the woes of a woman living alone in the city. Makan had made 'Bachelor Girls (the term favoured by brokers, landlords and housing societies), a documentary on the battle single women face in finding places to rent, that reflected Makan's personal story. 'Nobody wants to rent to single women,' she says. Though perhaps this grouse can be echoed by single men, queer persons or others not fitting the 'ideal' mould too as I have heard at so many different fora.

Kalpana Sharma says in this interview,[52] in the context of the book that she has edited, *Single by Choice*, 'There is a very big misconception that single women aren't contented, and that has been busted in many of the essays ... First of all, in India, it is very hard to be alone.' The organization *Ekal Nari Shakti Sanghathan* focuses on strengthening and organizing single women; and in doing so it acts as a pressure group lobbying with the government for better, more empowering policies for the single women.'[53]

Single men are burdened by their own share of woes. Writer Mayank Shekhar's tongue-in-cheek account of the man sans a woman negotiating the convoluted barriers that he peculiarly faces, gives a fresh perspective to being single. From being barred from nightclubs, to the tough competition from older, richer males for the few available women, to being seen as sleazy if he makes the 'first' move, life looks tough. And so he ends plaintively: Everybody loves the single woman. The world donates her its affection, attention, drinks, dinner ... re-tweets, roses on Rose Day ... She gifts them hope. Nobody loves a single man; not even the single man himself, and least of all the bouncer outside the club.[54]

The norms in the West, given its individuation and acceptance of personal choices undergoes a huge shift when the same set of desires for happiness and emotional fulfilment are tested in traditionally rooted countries like India. How society deals with it and what cushioning grounds it can provide for the anti-normative and the person who doesn't answer to set boxes – the one who embraces the different forms of 'singledom', would be a key test for the country to show its capability to embrace new ways of looking at life. The rise of singles and the deviations from the hetero-normative, though not seen as headline-making news, nevertheless has huge implications for India's future.

EPILOGUE

This book begins with a childhood memory, which remained festering in some visceral part of my emotional space. In time it grew and became the starting point to more observations, a more critical understanding of the unfolding of our most fascinating and celebrated event – the wedding.

And it led to the writing of this book.

The journey often traverses uneven turf. The celebratory union of the wedded couple – the central theme of the wedding, being entwined with certain practices, which reinforce the uneven power equations between the bride and the groom – dowry and *kanyadaan*, to name a few.

And yet, the book chronicles a changing reality, with a note of hope as it explores the churning of the social processes. The questioning has begun. We find fresh discourses in social media, academia, legal circles, the arts, the government, in television and entertainment, in areas inhabited by the youth – where individuals – both women and men are raising their voices, asking questions, demanding changes that would make a better world. A more equitable world. A diminished patriarchy. The backlash often follows, the news can be grim, but the good news is that the signs of positive changes are there. The recent Supreme Court rulings abolishing Article 377 is a case in point. The many references to the narratives of positivity I have made throughout the book are testimony to the freshness of the voices being raised. How this would translate in the years to come and the wedding scene in India, will be the litmus test that would shape India's social fabric for decades to come.

And so I am fast forwarding to circa 2040 – just a couple of decades from now – wherein a generational change would have been set in motion.

I imagine it would be something like this:

> A *baraat* that could have both the bridewallahs and the groomwallahs respectively, and meet on 'neutral grounds.' This would make a movie title like: *Dilwale Dulhaniya Le Jayenge* sound like an anachronism. Where the dowry quotations would not grease the path to arranging a match. Where parents trying to fix a match would not watch anxiously as their daughter came with a tray to serve the sherbet. And a couple would no longer need to follow the 'Love Laws', of whom to love and how much, so no runaway couples, no protection homes, no khap panchayats telling women not to use a mobile, or lawyers and judges giving moral science lessons to young 'mixed' couples. Where the youth don't turn to porn as an educative foray into learning about sex, where couples belonging to the LGBTQIA community feel safe, and single women and men don't have problems in finding a place to call their own … and so a land where we can hope in Tagore's words: 'Freedom from the burden of the ages, bending your head, breaking your back, blinding your eyes to the beckoning call of the future.'

NOTES

Preface

1. *Saptapadi* quite literally translates from Sanskrit to seven steps, as the couple take seven rounds of the sacred fire, to solemnize their marriage with accompanying vows. Traditionally, the bride's sari is tied to the groom's kurta, or a sari shawl might be draped from his shoulder to her sari. By walking around the fire they are agreeing to these vows. With each step, they throw small bits of puffed rice into the fire, representing prosperity in their new life together. This is considered the most important part of the ceremony, as it seals the bond between the couple forever.

   The following mantras are repeated as the couples take the seven sacred steps:

   1. May this couple be blessed with an abundance of resources and comforts, and be helpful to one another in all ways.
   2. May this couple be strong and complement one another.
   3. May this couple be blessed with prosperity and riches at all levels.
   4. May this couple be eternally happy.
   5. May this couple be blessed with a happy family life.
   6. May this couple live in perfect harmony ... true to their personal values and their joint promises.

7. May this couple always be the best of friends. See https://www.indiatoday.in/lifestyle/culture/story/hindu-wedding-rituals-ancient-traditions-indian-marriage-sacred-fire-lifest-1097231-2017-11-30

2. Ravinder Kaur and Rajni Palriwala (Eds.), *Marrying in South Asia, Shifting Concepts and Changing Practices in a Globalizing World*, Orient Blackswan, 2013.
3. Louis Dumont (1911-1998), an eminent French sociologist and Indologist, was a towering figure in the fields of sociology and anthropology. He wrote extensively on the Indian caste system and constructed exemplary research methodologies for the study of particular societies and for inter-civilizational comparison.
4. Nur Yalman is a leading Turkish social anthropologist at Harvard University, where he serves as Senior Research Professor of Social Anthropology and Middle Eastern Studies.
5. From the data released on marital status, it is observed that, at the national level, the proportion of currently married women to total number of women is reported to be 49.9 per cent in Census 2011 as against 47.7 per cent in Census 2001. In case of males it is 46 per cent in Census 2011 as against 43.6 per cent in Census 2001. See 'Census 2011 Data on Marital Status & Fertility & Head of Household Released', *Press Information Bureau*, 28 April 2015, https://pib.gov.in/newsite/mbErel.aspx?relid=119871.
6. Ibid.
7. As per Census 2011, youth (15–24 years) in India constitutes one-fifth (19.1 per cent) of India's total population. India is expected to have 34.33 per cent of youth in total population by 2020. See 'Youth in India', Ministry of Statistics and Programme Implementation, March 2017, http://mospi.nic.in/sites/default/files/publication_reports/Youth_in_India-2017.pdf.
8. Irawati Karve, 'The Kinship Map of India', *Family Kinship and Marriage in India*, Oxford University Press, 1993.
9. Promilla Kapur, *Love Marriage and Sex*, Vikas Publishing House, 1973.
10. Shastras are deeply philosophical ancient Hindu scriptures, which expound on life, death, karma, and ways of living.

There are Dharma Sutras, Smritis, Shrutis, Vedas, Upanishads, Brahmanas, Puranas etc.

11. The Ramayana, originally written by Rishi Valmiki on the lives of Sita and Rama, is one of the two major Hindu epics. It portrays Rama as the ideal man, who is also considered to be one of Vishnu's avatars. There are several other versions of it like Tulsidas's Ramcharitamanas, or the Tamil Kambaramayanam, a popular version, written by poet Kamban in the twelfth century. In Andhra Pradesh, Sri Ranganatha Ramayanam was adapted by Gona Budda Reddy. There are other versions in other countries.
12. Manu is a mythological figure, considered to be the eldest born of Lord Brahma. He compiled the Manusmriti, a detailed exegesis on the Hindu way of life. He is also known as the 'first king', and most rulers of medieval India traced their genealogy back to him. Manusmriti, translated as 'The Laws of Manu' or 'The Institutions of Manu', is an important Hindu Law Book (Dharmashastra), which served as a foundational work on Hindu law and jurisprudence in ancient India. See Jayaram V, 'Manusmriti the Laws of Manu – Introduction', *Hinduwebsite*, https://www.hinduwebsite.com/sacredscripts/hinduism/dharma/manusmriti.asp.
13. *Kanyadaan* – the giving of the daughter to the groom by the parents to the chanting of mantras – may have been inspired from the injunctions in the Manusmriti, where in *Brahma Vivah*, it is enjoined that the bride, bedecked and bejewelled, should be given away by her parents to a worthy groom.
14. The Kama Sutra is an ancient Indian text which is considered to be a canonical work on human sexuality. It was written by Mallanaga Vatsyayana in the second century CE.
15. Abhigyan Shakuntalam is a beautiful tale of love and romance, the name literally meaning 'Of Shakuntala who is recognized by a token'.
16. P.V. Narasimha Rao was an Indian lawyer and politician who served as the prime minister of India (1991–1996). Along with

his then Finance Minister Manmohan Singh, he carried out several structural reforms that liberalized India's economy.

17. 'BJP MLA's Daughter Says Father Wants To Kill Her For Marrying Dalit Man', Huffpost, 11 July 2019, https://www.huffingtonpost.in/entry/bjp-mla-daughter-alleges- threat-to-life-for-marrying-dalit-man_in_5d26e3e2e4 b0cfb59600b259.
18. Prem Chowdhry, *Contentious Marriages, Eloping Couples, Gender, Caste, and Patriarchy in Northern India*, Oxford University Press, 2007.
19. *Shringar rasa* is one of the nine *rasas* that define all Indian art forms. *Shringar rasa* imbues the twin moods of love, *milan* or togetherness and *viyog* or the sorrow of separation.
20. The Taj Wedding Barometer, a survey conducted by Taj Group of Hotels in 2013. The survey conducted by IPSOS of some 1,000 young people across ten cities showed that 84 per cent people in north India prefer arranged marriage.
21. 'Indians Swear by Arranged Marriages', *India Today*, 4 March 2013, http://indiatoday.intoday.in/story/indians-swear-by-arranged-marriages/1/252496.html
22. To understand how young Indians look at planning their own wedding, Matrimony.com undertook The Big Fat Indian Wedding Market Survey 2018, in which 9,246 people all over India participated online. According to a KPMG report published in 2014, the wedding services market is estimated to be around $54 billion.
23. Sex Ratio Imbalances and Marriage Squeeze in India: 2000–2050. Paper One. This is the first in a three-paper series prepared for United Nations Population Fund By Ravinder Kaur Surjit, S. Bhalla, Manoj K. Agarwal and Prasanthi Ramakrishnan, https://india.unfpa.org/sites/default/files/pub-pdf/Sex%20Ratio%20Imbalances%20and%20Marriage%20Squeeze.pdf
24. Henrike Donner, *Domestic Goddesses: Maternity, Globalization and Middle-class Identity in Contemporary India*, Routledge, 2008.
25. 'Indians Swear by Arranged Marriages', *India Today*, 4 March 2013, http://indiatoday.intoday.in/story/indians-swear-by-arranged-marriages/1/252496.html.

26. Bhartrihari was a Hindu philosopher and poet-grammarian in Ujjayini around the sixth century BC.
27. On 6 September 2018, the Supreme Court of India ruled unanimously in Navtej Singh Johar v. Union of India that Section 377 was unconstitutional 'in so far as it criminalizes consensual sexual conduct between adults of the same sex'.

1. Toeing the Line: Marriage as a Life Changer

1. Dharma Shastras or Hindu law books mention four *ashrams* or stages of human life: *Brahmacharya* or stage of being a celibate student, *Grihasth* ashram or stage of living as a householder, *Vanaprastha ashram* or stage of dwelling in the forests, and *Sanyas ashram* or the stage of renunciation and spirituality.
2. Betwa Sharma, 'Indian gay men's wives "trapped" in marriage', *Al Jazeera*, 22 August 2014, https://www.aljazeera.com/indepth/features/2014/08/indian-gay-men-wives-trapped-marriage-201482261281 11437.html.
3. Gowthaman Ranganathan, 'Forced into Marriage by Social Pressures', Alternative Law Forum, 30 April 2015, http://altlawforum.org/publications/forced-into-marriage-by-social-pressures/.
4. Friedrich Engels (1820–1895) was a German political philosopher, who collaborated closely with Karl Marx in the foundation of modern Communism. *The Origin of the Family, Private Property, and the State* (1884) is a detailed seminal work connecting the development of capitalism with what Engels argues is an unnatural institution, the family, which is designed to 'privatize' wealth and human relationships against the way in which animals and early humans naturally evolved. It contains a comprehensive historical view of the family in relation to the issues of social class, female subjugation and ownership of private property.
5. George Steinmetz (Ed.), *State/Culture: State-Formation after the Cultural Turn*, Cornell University Press, 1999.

6. Johann Jakob Bachofen (1815–1887) was a Swiss anthropologist and sociologist, famous for his theory of matriarchy and his work on the role of women in ancient societies.
7. Joseph Veroff and Shela Feld, *Marriage and Work in America: A Study of Motives and Roles*, Van Nostrand Reinhold Co., 1970.
8. The Vedas are considered the earliest literary record of Indo-Aryan civilization and the most sacred books of India. They are scriptures of Hindu teachings, containing spiritual knowledge encompassing all aspects of life. The four Vedas are: Rig Veda, Sama Veda, Atharva Veda and Yajur Veda.

   The Puranas are estimated to have been written between the fourth century BC and the eleventh century BC. They contain myths and genealogies, and expound on a range of subjects like religious rituals, duties and developments.
9. Anushashan Parva is the thirteenth parva of Mahabharata and it comprises of two sub-parvas. It consists of the final instructions given by Bhishma, as he lies dying on his bed of arrows in the battlefield, to Yudhishthira, the eldest of the Pandavas.
10. The Rig Veda is a collection of inspired songs or hymns, and is the main source of information on the Vedic civilization. It is the oldest book in any Indo-European language and contains the earliest form of all Sanskrit mantras that date back to 1500 BC–1000 BC.
11. Kaal Chiron, 'Brief history of Hindu Marriage - 1 - Evolution of Human Pair Bonding as seen from Puranas and Vedas', 3 April 2012, *Kaal – Chiron*, http://kalchiron.blogspot.in/2012/04/brief-history-of-hindu-marriage-1.html.
12. Devdutt Pattanaik, 'The Strange Tale of Oghavati', *Devdutt*, 10 June 2011, http://devdutt.com/articles/indian-mythology/mahabharata/the-strange-tale-of-oghavati.html.
13. Sarvepalli Radhakrishnan, *Religion and Society*, George Allen & Unwin Ltd, 1956.
14. Swami Vivekananda, *Complete Works of Swami Vivekananda*, Advaita Ashram Vol 4, 1946.

15. Promilla Kapur, *Love, Marriage and Sex*, Vikas Publishing House, 1973.
16. Pierre Bourdieu, *Masculine Domination*, Polity Press, 2001.
17. Pierre Bourdieu and Loïc Wacquant, *An Invitation to Reflexive Sociology*, Polity Press, 1992.
18. Clare Chambers, *Sex, Culture and Justice: The Limits of Choice*, Pennsylvania State University Press, 2008.
19. Anne Kingston, *The Meaning of Wife*, Piatkus, 2004.
20. Karwa chauth is ritualistic fasting through the day by women for the well-being and long life of their husbands. The fast is broken in the evening once the moon is sighted.
21. Deepali Nandwani, 'The recession-proof Big Fast Indian Wedding just got more corporatised', CNBC TV18, 8 October 2018, https://www.cnbctv18.com/retail/the-recession-proof-big-fast-indian-wedding-just-got-more-corporatised-1012991.htm.

2. Arranging Love

1. 'Indians Swear by Arranged Marriages', *India Today*, 4 March 2013, http://indiatoday.intoday.in/story/indians-swear-by-arranged-marriages/1/252496.html.
2. Sudhir Kakar and Katharina Kakar, *The Indians: Portrait of a People*, Penguin, 2007.
3. 'PM Narendra Modi's Independence Day speech at the Red Fort: Highlights', *The Economic Times*, 16 August 2014, https://economictimes.indiatimes.com/news/politics-and-nation/pm-narendra-modis-independence-day-speech-at-the-red-fort-highlights/articleshow/40308036.cms.
4. Shiva Devnath, 'Mumbai: Couples picked up from hotel rooms, charged with 'public indecency', *Mid-Day*, 8 August 2015, http://www.mid-day.com/articles/mumbai-couples-picked-up-from-hotel-rooms-charged-with-public-indecency/16437186.
5. 'Indore Police Thrash 'Couples' Sitting in Park', *Daily Bhaskar*, 5 August 2013, https://daily.bhaskar.com/news/MP-IND-police-

makes-mockery-of-law-openly-thrashes-boys-and-girls-sitting-in-regional-p-4305012-PHO.html.

6. Gayatri Gauri, 'Masaan review: This Cannes winner is a beautiful and poignant portrait of small-town India', *Firstpost*, 24 July 2015, http://www.firstpost.com/bollywood/masaan-review-this-cannes-winner-is-a-beautiful-and-poignant-portrait-of-small-town-india-2358906.html.
7. Ravinder Kaur with Preeti Dhanda, 'Surfing for Spouses: Marriage websites and the 'new' Indian Marriage?', *Marrying in South Asia*, Orient Blackswan, 2014.
8. Mukta Sharangpani, 'Browsing for Bridegrooms: Matchmaking and Modernity in Mumbai', *Indian Journal of Gender Studies*, 2010.
9. Devaki Jain and Nirmala Banerjee, *The Tyranny of the Household*, Vikas Publishing House, 1985.
10. Abhijit Banerji, Esther Duflo, Maitreesh Ghatak and Jeanne LaFortune, 'Marry for What? Caste and Mate Selection in Modern India', *American Economic Journal: Microeconomics*, May 2013, https://economics.mit.edu/files/8979.
11. A recent survey conducted online by the marriage portal Shaadi.com for the duration of four months. Over 1.5 lakh respondents from India and Non-Resident Indians from the UK, US, Canada, Middle East, South East Asia, Australia and New Zealand participated in this survey. More young Indians are keen on staying in a joint family – 54 per cent of females and 53 per cent of males. On the other hand, 69 per cent women wanted their husbands to be more educated than them. Being fair, as it seems, has its own advantages if you're a single woman looking to get married. According to the survey results, 49 per cent of men expect a 'fair and lovely' looking woman as their partner as compared to just 25 per cent women who were keen that their man have a fair complexion.
12. Pavan K. Verma, *Being Indian: The Truth About Why the Twenty-first Century Will be India's*, Arrow Books, 2006.
13. Clare Chambers, 'Feminism, Liberalism and Marriage', *Presented at*

Annual Meeting of the American Political Science Association in Washington DC, 2012.

14. http://www.statista.com/topics/2157/internet-usage-in-india/; https://economictimes.indiatimes.com/tech/software/how-online-dating-companies-make-money-in-india/articleshow/65759943.cms.
    According to online market researcher Statista, Indian online dating companies are expected to earn around $13 million in 2018, with nearly half the singles (41 million) from the 2011 census on dating apps by 2022. Statista also says sectoral revenue is expected to show a compounded annual growth rate of 10.3 per cent over the next four years, which would result in a market volume of $20 million by 2022.
15. 'Case Study: How Shaadi.com became leader in the online matrimonial industry?', Delhi School of Internet Marketing, 8 June 2016, https://dsim.in/blog/2016/06/08/case-study-how-shaadi-com-started-as-an-experiment-became-leader-in-the-online-matrimonial-industry/.
16. Sycorian is an online matrimonial site that claims on its website: we have a proficient knowledge regarding the hospitality industry, public relations, international and local trading and fund management act which often turn out to be remarkably beneficial for our clients.
17. Surfing for Spouses, Marriage Websites and the 'New'Indian Marriage? Ravinder Kaur with Preeti Dhanda Marrying in South Asia: Shifting concepts, Changing Practices in a Globalsing World. Eds Ravinder Kaur and Rajni Palriwala, published by Orient Blackswan.
18. Anthony Giddens is one of the major contemporary sociological theorists. In his book, *Dilemmas of the Self*, Giddens examines four seemingly contradictory aspects of contemporary modern society. Each of these dilemmas can lead to pathological results for an individual; at the same time, each dilemma opens new possibilities and opportunities for an individual, possibilities that

can be creative and produce a better life. He has the most sophisticated way of connecting a microsociological theory of social action with a macrosociological explanation of the systems and structures of society.

19. https://www.statista.com/topics/2157/internet-usage-in-india/
20. In the *gotra* system a person is identified by his or her most ancient ancestor in an unbroken male lineage.
21. 'Online Matrimonial Sites and Transformation of Arranged Marriage in India' by Naynika Seth and Ravi Patnayankuni, University of Alabama in Huntsville USA. https://www.researchgate.net/publication/266908028_Online_Matrimonial_Sites_and_the_Transformation_of_Arranged_Marriage_in_India; also see https://www.statista.com/statistics/750999/india-share-of-internet-users-by-gender/.
22. Suneera Tandon, 'India's rural internet users love Facebook, WhatsApp, and free music downloads', *Quartz India*, 12 August 2016, https://qz.com/india/755825/anatomy-of-a-rural-internet-user-in-india/.
23. 'India's youth prefer communicating through social networks: Report', *NDTV*, 17 June 2013, https://gadgets.ndtv.com/social-networking/news/indias-youth-prefer-communicating-through-social-networks-report-380453.
24. Rina Chandran, 'Indian villages ban single women from owning 'distracting' mobile phones', *Reuters*, 26 February 2016, https://www.reuters.com/article/us-india-women-phone-idUSKCN0VZ1AA.

3. Weddings and the Kiss of Money

1. Parvati, also known as Mother Goddess, is one of the incarnations of Shakti, and Lord Shiva's consort. They are together seen as the ideal couple in the Hindu pantheon.
2. Sanjay Jha and Flora Drury, 'My big fat £15 million wedding: Hinduja tycoon and his designer bride marry in stunning Bollywood ceremony complete with entertainment from J-Lo

and Nicole Scherzinger', *The Daily Mail*, 13 February 2015, https://www.dailymail.co.uk/news/article-2952115/Hinduja-tycoon-designer-bride-marry-stunning-Bollywood-ceremony-complete-entertainment-J-Lo-Nicole-Scherzinger.html.

3. 'All You Need to Know about Grand Wedding of Richest Indian Billionaire's Daughter Isha Ambani', Indian Eagle, https://www.indianeagle.com/travelbeats/isha-ambani-wedding-details/.
4. Niha Masih and Shashank Bengali, 'Must Reads: India's richest man throws the wedding to end all weddings, with Beyonce and Hillary in attendance', *Los Angeles Times*, 13 December 2018, https://www.latimes.com/world/la-fg-india-ambani-wedding-20181213-story.html.
5. 'Cabinet nod to Rs 1 lakh cr for urban renewal, 100 smart cities to take off', *Business Standard*, 9 July 2015, www.business-standard.com/article/economy-policy/cabinet-nod-to-rs-1-lakh-cr-for-urban-renewal-100-smart-cities-to-take-off-115042900832_1.html.
6. Alice Newbold, 'Everything You Need To Know About Priyanka Chopra & Nick Jonas's Wedding', *Vogue*, 3 January 2019, https://www.vogue.co.uk/article/priyanka-chopra-wedding-news-pictures.
7. Pepsi's ad campaign 'Yeh Dil Maange More!' resonated deeply across the country that was waking up to a consumer revolution, a move from a command-driven economy to a demand-driven economy. So, Indians were now not settling for any car or any TV or any soft drink. See Ambi Parameswaran, 'Out With the Old, More of the New', *The Indian Express*, 24 July 2016, http://indianexpress.com/article/business/business-others/out-with-the-old-more-of-the-new-2932688/.
8. Imran Ahmed, 'Inside India's Big Fat $38 Billion Wedding Market', *Business of Fashion*, 7 August 2013, https://www.businessoffashion.com/articles/global-currents/inside-indias-big-fat-38-billion-wedding-market-part-1-rohit-bal-sabyasachi-mukherjee-alex-kuruvilla-vijay-singh-india-bridal-fashion-week.
9. 'Indian politician's £14m wedding for his son... complete with

18,000 guests and a replica Rajasthani palace', *The Daily Mail*, 4 March 2011, http://www.dailymail.co.uk/news/article-1363056/Indian-politicians-14m-wedding-son--complete-18-000-guests-replica-Rajastani-palace.html#ixzz3ov2WrCoI.

10. Quoting Sabyasachi Mukherjee: 'The bridal market is a great example of the trickle-down theory. Since weddings are the apex of fashion and spending, what's designed for weddings will trickle down the market as festive wear and then high-street clothing. While fashion prides itself on being democratic, there is no doubt that its elitist elements give it sheen and allure. And for now, in India, fashion depends on weddings to create a feeling of fantasy.'
11. https://www.kotak.com/content/dam/Kotak/about-us/media-press-releases/2018/seventh-edition-of-top-of-the-pyramid-report.pdf.
12. Fflur Roberts, 'Predictions for the Luxury Goods Industry in 2015', *Luxury Society*, 19 January 2015, https://www.luxurysociety.com/en/articles/2015/01/20-predictions-for-the-luxury-goods-industry-in-2015/.
13. The Hindu Succession (Amendment) Act, 2005 (39 of 2005) came into force from 9 September, 2005. The Amendment removes gender discriminatory provisions in the Hindu Succession Act, 1956.
14. Janaki Fernandes, 'Chit fund scam: How Saradha duped its investors', *NDTV*, 24 April 2013, http://www.ndtv.com/india-news/chit-fund-scam-how-saradha-duped-its-investors-520076.
15. Shailaja Chandra, 'Dhoom-dham of shaadis', *over2shailaja*, 1 May 2010, http://over2shailaja.wordpress.com/tag/ostentatious-weddings/.
16. Santosh Tiwari, 'Black money estimated at 30% of GDP', *Business Standard*, 29 January 2013, https://www.business-standard.com/article/economy-policy/black-money-estimated-at-30-of-gdp-113011300067_1.html.
17. An average Indian wedding could cost between ₹20 lakhs to 5 crores; translating to a person spending almost one-fifth

of their total wealth accumulated in their lifetime on their wedding. https://economictimes.indiatimes.com/tdmc/your-money/navigation/financial-planning/save-invest/destination-weddings-or-luxury-honeymoons-cost-analysis-to-help-you-decide/articleshow/71645023.cms?from=mdr

18. Francis Bloch, Vijayendra Rao and Sonalde Desai, 'Wedding Celebrations as Conspicuous Consumption: Signaling Social Status in Rural India', *The Journal of Human Resources*, 2004.
19. James Heitzman and Robert L. Worden, *India: A Country Study*, The Library of Congress, 1995.
20. M.N. Srinivas, *Village, Caste, Gender, and Method: Essays in Indian Social Anthropology*, Oxford University Press, 1998.
21. Sonalde Desai, 'Wedding Celebrations as Conspicuous Consumption: Signaling Social Status in Rural India', *Journal of Human Resources*, June 2004.
22. Inspired by Bollywood celebrities, young singles want destination weddings: Survey, Published: 20 December 2018, https://www.newindianexpress.com/nation/2018/dec/20/rahul-gandhi-faces-delhi-bjp-fire-over-rafale-jet-deal-1913944.html. Also see 'Indian Hospitality Woos Destination Wedding Industry,' https://www.entrepreneur.com/article/332959.
23. Brett Arends, 'Mega-Weddings: Why You Should Say 'I Don't', *The Wall Street Journal*, 3 October 2014, https://www.wsj.com/articles/mega-weddings-why-you-should-say-i-dont-1412349202.

4. Bollywood Masala

1. India has been the largest movie producer worldwide for the last few years, releasing more than a thousand films each year. There were two thousand multiplex theaters in India as of 2015. A year later, more than 2.2 billion movie tickets were sold in India, placing the country as the leading film market in the world. In the 2019 fiscal year, the Indian film industry was valued at over 180 billion Indian rupees. According to industry experts, it was

estimated to reach up to 260 billion rupees by the fiscal year of 2024.
https://www.statista.com/topics/2140/film-industry-in-india/.

2. As per a FICCI-EY report, 'despite comprising only 17 per cent of the films made in the country, Bollywood contributes almost 40 per cent to the net box office collections annually. Films made in almost 29 other Indian languages contribute around 75 per cent of the films released but they contribute approximately 50 per cent to the annual domestic box office collections. The balance is constituted from Hollywood and international films.'
https://www.businesstoday.in/opinion/columns/how-indian-cinema-evolved-into-being-one-of-the-most-powerful-modes-of-entertainment/story/307454.html.
3. The first available text, dealing entirely with stagecraft (including dance and music) is Natya Shastra, the original portions of the revered treatise were written by Bharata Muni, a sage. It has also been called the 'Fifth Veda', because of its importance. Though it has been dated between 200 BC and 200 AD, the date of Natya Shastra is a big controversy. It is a text that has grown over centuries but it is not possible to point out which lines or portions are later additions. But it is believed to precede Valmiki's Ramayana by scholars, as it is evident from the oldest portions like the Sunder and Yuddha Kandas that Valmiki was using Bharat Muni's terminology with a musicological awareness. Mention of many aspects of Indian classical music of today can be found in Natya Shastra.
Kapila Vatsyayan, *Bharata: The Natyasastra*, Sahitya Akademi, New Delhi,1996.
4. Rachel Dwyer, *Bollywood India: Hindi Cinema as a Guide to Contemporary India*, Reaktion Books, 2014.
5. To quote sociologist Sudhir Kakar, 'Watched by almost 15 million people every day, popular cinema's values and language ... have begun to influence Indian ideas of the good life and the ideology of social, family and love relationships.'

6. Tejaswini Ganti, *Producing Bollywood: Inside the Contemporary Hindi Film Industry*, Duke University Press, 2012.
7. Patricia Uberoi, 'Imagining the Family: An Ethnography of viewing *Hum Aapke Hain Kaun*', *The Bollywood Reader*, McGraw Hill Open University Press, 2008.
8. Monika Mehta, 'Globalizing Bombay Cinema: Reproducing the Indian State and Family', *Cultural Dynamics*, SAGE Publications, 2005.
9. https://boxofficeindia.com/movie.php?movieid=11
10. Uberoi (n 7).
11. 85 per cent Indians prefer to marry the boy or girl chosen by their families, rather than choosing their life partners themselves. This statistic was revealed in a survey conducted by the Taj Group of Hotels. Another survey by IPSOS in 2013, revealed that 74 per cent of young Indians, aged between 18–35 years said that they would rather let their parents choose their life partners, than choosing themselves. See https://www.culturalindia.net/weddings/arranged-marriage.html; https://medium.com/@solutionswebomania/current-trends-arranged-marriages-in-india-e0435d455e8e
12. https://movies.ndtv.com/bollywood/the-end-maratha-mandir-shows-dilwale-dulhania-le-jayenge-for-last-time-740769
13. Santosh Desai, *Mother Pious Lady: Making Sense of Everyday India*, Harper Collins, 2010.
14. Roshmila Bhattacharya, '1,300 cases of groom kidnapping were registered last year', *Hindustan Times*, 25 August 2010, https://www.hindustantimes.com/bollywood/1-300-cases-of-groom-kidnapping-were-registered-last-year/story-aOMbfgFmPxhRMOp4FkXAZI.html.
15. As early as 1993, the magazine *India Today* reported such kidnappings by 'social groups', one of which had formed in 1982 in Bihar, to kidnap grooms who demanded heavy dowries and forcibly marry them. In some cases, if the groom asks for too large a dowry or backs out of a marriage owing to dowry issues, the girl's family resorts to such measures, having the groom abducted via criminal gangs.

5. Breaking Love's Barriers

1. *Gotra* – Exogamous patrilineal clan where members claim descent from a particular sage. The sons inherit their father's *gotra* and daughters once married take on their husband's *gotra*.
2. 'Supreme Court Says Khap Panchayats Illegal, No Assembly Can Interfare In A Marriage Between Two Consenting Adults', *Outlook*, 27 March 2018, https://www.outlookindia.com/website/story/supreme-court-declares-khap-panchayats-illegal/310063.
3. Suruchi Thapar-Björkert and Gurchathen Sanghera, 'The Ascendancy of the Khap Panchayats in Contemporary India: Gender, Caste, Globalisation and Violence', *Intersections: Gender and Sexuality in Asia and the Pacific*, March 2014, http://intersections.anu.edu.au/issue34/thapar-bjorkert_sanghera.htm.
4. 'Violence around inter-caste marriage' by Prem Chowdhry 17 July 2019' https://www.tribuneindia.com/news/comment/violence-around-inter-caste-marriages/803140.html
5. 'Regressive Khap Panchayat Rulings That Dragged India Backwards To The Stone Ages,' https://www.scoopwhoop.com/regressive-rulings-by-khap-panchayats/.
6. 'Death sentence commuted in Manoj-Babli case', *The Hindu*, 12 March 2011, https://www.thehindu.com/news/national/Death-sentence-commuted-in-Manoj-Babli-case/article14943294.ece.
7. 'I loved Rizwan, Priyanka Todi tells CBI', *Zee News*, 1 November 2007, http://zeenews.india.com/news/nation/i-loved-rizwan-priyanka-todi-tells-cbi_404840.html.
8. Suryatapa Bhattacharya, 'Relationships gone wrong accounted for the third highest number of murders in 2012', *The National*, 18 September 2013, https://www.thenational.ae/world/1.338563.
9. Nivedita Menon, 'Sexuality, Caste, Governmentality: Contests Over "Gender" in India', *Feminist Review*, 2009.
10. The love story of Prithviraj Chauhan and Sangyogita is a popular tragic romance that has become as much part of the Indian folklore as the legends of Heer-Ranjha or Sohni-Maliwal. The

twelfth-century king's love story was immortalized by his court poet Chand Bardai in his epic poem *Prithviraj Raso*.

11. 'More than 1,000 honour killings in India every year: Experts', *The Times of India*, 4 July 2010, http://timesofindia.indiatimes.com/india/More-than-1000-honour-killings-in-India-every-year-Experts/articleshow/6127338.cms.
12. Ankita Chaurasia, 'Sawantwadi: Haven for instant weddings!', *The Free Press Journal*, 15 January 2017, https://www.freepressjournal.in/cmcm/sawantwadi-haven-for-instant-weddings.
13. Meena Dhanda, 'Runaway Marriages A Silent Revolution?', *Economic & Political Weekly*, 27 October 2012.
14. Prem Chowdhry, *Contentious Marriages, Eloping Couples: Gender, Caste, and Patriarchy in Northern India*, Oxford University Press, 2007.
15. Census 2011. Punjab has 893 females to 1000 males and Haryana, the lowest figures in the country at 877: 1000 (2011)
16. Dhanda (n 13).
17. Ajay Sura, 'HC advises runaway couples to follow social norms', *The Times of India*, 10 June 2015, http://timesofindia.indiatimes.com/city/chandigarh/HC-advises-runaway-couples-to-follow-social-norms/articleshow/47608280.cms.
18. Chowdhry (n 14).
19. 'After BJP MLA's daughter Sakshi Misra, more UP couples seek police protection', *India Today*, 28 June 2019, https://www.indiatoday.in/india/story/after-bjp-mla-s-daughter-sakshi-misra-more-up-couples-seek-police-protection-1574451-2019-07-28.
20. Shiva Devnath, 'Mumbai: Couples picked up from hotel rooms, charged with 'public indecency', *Mid-Day*, 8 August 2015, http://www.mid-day.com/articles/mumbai-couples-picked-up-from-hotel-rooms-charged-with-public-indecency/16437186.
21. Sudhir Kakar and Katharina Kakar, *The Indians: Portrait of a People*, Penguin, 2007.
22. Gandharva marriage (the marriage of the celestials) is one of the eight types of Hindu marriages. Gandharva marriage is a form of love marriage.

23. The Youth Study was the first-ever sub-national, representative study of youth in India. Its objectives were to identify key transitions experienced by youth, including those pertaining to education, work-force participation, sexual activity, marriage, health and civic participation; provide state-level evidence on the magnitude and patterns of young people's sexual and reproductive practices in and outside of marriage, as well as related knowledge, decision-making and attitudes; and, finally, identify key factors underlying young people's sexual and reproductive health knowledge, attitudes and life choices.
24. https://www.outlookindia.com/magazine/story/business-news-politicians-more-dangerous-than-terrorists-youth-survey-reveals-startling-details/301729
25. 'Sex Survey 2019: Small towns getting bolder with their sexual choices', https://www.indiatoday.in/lifestyle/what-s-hot/story/survey-2019-small-towns-getting-bolder-with-their-choices-1614729-2019-11-01
26. Vitamin Stree, a young, video-first content platform in the business of reshaping the narrative for young women in India, has produced this paper based on the findings of a sex survey they conducted with urban millennials in India in 2018. They conducted an online survey with 2,500 young women and men to find about their views on sex and sexuality. They were between the ages of 18 and 35 years. 1,632 identified as female and 728 as male, and of this group, a majority identified as heterosexual, 235 identified as bisexual and 66 identified as homosexuals. See vitaminstree.com/censexwhitepaper, https://www.youthkiawaaz.com/2019/02/censex-the-vitamin-stree-sex-survey/
27. 'Final Report Study on Counter Magnet Areas to Delhi & NCR', *National Capital Region Planning Board CMA Study*, 2008, http://ncrpb.nic.in/cma_study.html.
28. SECRT Sex Education Counselling Research Training and Therapy Department of the Family Planning Association of India. The study covers a sample of about 3,850 educated, unmarried boys

and girls between 15 and 29 years of age, in selected areas in all the four regions - North, South, East and West. The results indicate that the attitudes of the young people in all the four regions towards marriage and sexuality are more or less the same. The high percentage of non-responses also point to the fact that few young people have given any advance thought to their sexual behaviour and its consequences, particularly at the time of entering into marriage.

29. vitaminstree.com/censexwhitepaper, https://www.youthkiawaaz.com/2019/02/censex-the-vitamin-stree-sex-survey/
30. 'Health behaviours & problems among young people in India', https://www.ncbi.nlm.nih.gov › pmc › articles › PMC4216492.

6. The Devil is in the Dowry

1. Dowries originally started as 'love' gifts after the marriages of upper caste individuals, but during the medieval period the demands for dowries became a precursor for marriage. Stanley J. Tambiah claims the ancient Code of Manu sanctioned dowry and bride wealth in ancient India, but dowry was the more prestigious form and associated with the Brahmanic (priestly) caste. Bride wealth was restricted to the lower castes, who were not allowed to give dowry. See Prakasa Rao, *Marriage, The Family and Women in India*, South Asia Books, 1982.
2. *Streedhan* – Gifts made to a woman before the nuptial fire; gifts made at the bridal procession; gifts made by father-in-law, mother-in-law; by father, mother and brother; gifts made after marriage by a woman's husband's relations or parent's relations and gifts from sons and relations too form the *streedhan*. It is a voluntary gift given by members of the bridal side to the bride as a stepping-stone to establishing her own property. https://www.lawctopus.com/academike/streedhan-right-woman/
3. Veena Talwar Oldenburg, *Dowry Murder: The Imperial Origins of a Cultural Crime*, Oxford University Press, 2002.

4. Ursula Sharma, *Women, Work & Property in North West India*, Tavistock Publications, 1980.
5. As per Census 2011, gender ratio of India is 943 females per 1000 males. Sex ratio of India is 107.48, i.e. 107.48 males per 100 females in 2019. It means that India has 930 females per 1000 males. In absolute terms, India has 48.20 per cent female population compared to 51.80 per cent male population. India has 4,93,14,062 more males than females. India ranks 191 out of 201 countries in terms of female to male ratio. Among Asian countries, India ranks 43 out of 51. See Ministry of Statistics and Programme Implementation, 16 May 2019.
6. 'Gender and Son Meta-Preference: Is Development Itself an Antidote?', *Economic Survey 2017-2018 Volume 1*, Ministry of Finance, http://mofapp.nic.in:8080/economicsurvey/pdf/102-118_Chapter_07_ENGLISH_Vol_01_2017-18.pdf.
7. Ira Trivedi, 'A Generation of Girls Is Missing in India', *Foreign Policy*, 15 August 2019, https://foreignpolicy.com/2019/08/15/a-generation-of-girls-is-missing-in-india/.
8. Padma Srinivasan and Gary R. Lee, 'The dowry system in Northern India: Women's attitudes and social change', *Journal of Marriage and Family*, 2004.
9. Sonalde Desai and Lester Andrist, 'Gender Scripts and Age at Marriage in India', *Demography*, August 2010.
10. Srinivasan and Lee (n 8).
11. Meera Sundararajan, 'The Bridegroom Bazaar', 18 February 2011, http://meerareflections.blogspot.com/2011/02/bridegroom-bazaar.html
12. Ursula Sharma, 'Dowry In North India: Its Consequences for Women', *Family, Kinship and Marriage in India*, Oxford University Press, 1993.
13. Bina Agarwal, *A Field of One's Own: Gender and Land Rights in South Asia*, Cambridge University Press, 1995.
14. Srimati Basu, *She Comes to Take Her Rights: Indian Women, Property and Propriety*, SUNY Press, 1999.

15. Madhu Kishwar and Ruth Vanita (ed.), *Manushi: Voices of Indian Women's Liberation*, Banner Press, 1993.
16. Francis Bloch and Vijayendra Rao, 'Terror as a Bargaining Instrument: A Case Study of Dowry Violence in Rural India', *The World Bank Development Research Group Poverty and Human Resources*, 2000.
17. Madhu Purnima Kishwar, *Zealous Reformers and Deadly Laws*, Sage India, 2008.
18. Sonali Das, Sonali Jain-Chandra, Kalpana Kochhar and Naresh Kumar, '*Women Workers in India: Why So Few Among So Many?*', IMF *Working Paper no.* 15/55, 16 March 2015.
19. Conor Friedersdorf, 'Why PepsiCo CEO Indra K. Nooyi Can't Have It All', *The Atlantic*, 1 July 2014, https://www.theatlantic.com/business/archive/2014/07/why-pepsico-ceo-indra-k-nooyi-cant-have-it-all/373750/.
20. Sharma (n 12).
21. M.N. Srinivas, 'Some Reflections on Dowry', *Village, Caste, Gender and Method: Essays in Indian Social Anthropology*, Oxford University Press, 1997.

7. The Singular Life: Marriage From The Other Side

1. Recorded in Swami Satyananda Saraswati's sermon at BSY Monghyr in December 1980, http://www.yogamag.net/archives/1981/joct81/brahcha.shtml.
2. Sri Swami Sivananda, *Practice of Brahmacharya*, The Divine Life Society Publication, 1997.
3. 'Asceticism', Encyclopædia Britannica, 20 June 2013, https://www.britannica.com/topic/asceticism.
4. Alexandra Sifferlin, 'Can Sex Really Dampen Athletic Performance?', TIME, 23 June 2014, http://time.com/ 2911744/can-sex-really-dampen-athletic-performance/.
5. Eliana Dockterman, 'World Cup: The Crazy Rules Some Teams Have About Pre-Game Sex', 18 June 2014, https://time.com/2894263/world-cup-sex-soccer/.

6. Belinda Goldsmith and Kate Kale, 'No evidence that sex spoils sport', *Reuters*, 30 July 2012, http://www.reuters.com/article/2012/07/30/us-oly-sex-day-idusbre86t0tw20120730#9zh5jt4jf0ftlygx.97.
7. Catherine Clementine Ojha, 'Outside the Norms: Women Ascetics in Hindu Society, *Economic and Political Weekly*, 1988.
8. Arvind Sharma (ed.), *Women and Religion*, SUNY, 1987.
9. Nancy Auer Falk and Rita M. Gross (eds.), *Unspoken Worlds: Women's Religious Lives*, Wadsworth, 1989.
10. Sondra L. Hausner and Ann Grodzins Gold (eds.), *Nuns, Yoginis, Saints and Singers: Women's Renunciation in South Asia*, Zubaan, 2007.
11. Marie-Thérèse Charpentier, '*Indian Female Gurus in Contemporary Hinduism: A Study of Central Aspects and Expressions of Their Religious Leadership*', Åbo Akademi University Press, 2010.
12. Manisha Sethi, *Escaping the World: Women Renouncers among Jains*, Routledge, 2011.
13. 'Over 40 and loving it', https://www.theguardian.com/books/booksblog/2019/jun/28/over-40-loving-it-celebrate-fiction-positive-older-characters.
14. *Ageing Women in Literature and Visual Culture: Reflections, Refractions, Reimaginings*, McGlynn, Cathy, O'Neill, Margaret, Schrage-Früh, Michaela (Eds.), Springer, 2017; Making the Invisible Visible: The Presence of Older Women Artists in Early Modern Artistic Biography by Dabbs, Julia K., Palgrave Macmillan, 2017.
15. pass the bucket Good Morning Britain's Piers Morgan calls for ... https://www.thesun.co.uk › tvandshowbiz › good-morning-britains-piers-...
16. Madonna Woman of The Year Full Speech | Billboard Women in Music 2016, https://www.youtube.com/watch?v=c6Xgbh2E0NM.
17. https://www.hollywoodreporter.com/news/juliette-binoche-playing-an-older-woman-looking-love-let-sunshine-1108242
18. https://www.nytimes.com/2019/01/08/style/women-age-glenn-close.html

19. Jane Marple, usually referred to as Miss Marple, is a fictional character appearing in Agatha Christie's crime novels and in twenty short stories. Miss Marple is an elderly spinster and an amateur consulting detective. Alongside Hercule Poirot, she is one of the most loved and famous of Christie's characters and has been portrayed numerous times on screen.
20. The Natya Shastra is an ancient Indian treatise on the performing arts, primarily dealing with theatre, dance and music, but it has come to influence literature, makeup, stage design and virtually every other aspect of stagecraft.
21. Manusmriti in verses 3.55-3.56, *Manu's Code of Law* , translated and edited by Patrick Olivelle and Suman Olivelle, Oxford University Press, 2005.
22. Jyoti Sabharwal and Rita Ganguly, *Ae Mohabbat: Reminiscing Begum Akhtar*, Stellar Publishers, 2008.
23. E. Kay Trimberger, 'Single Women in India: Rarer, Riskier, and Happier Than in the U.S', *Unmarried Equality*, 2008.
24. Ibid.
25. Saanya Gulati, 'How Patriarchy Dictates When An Indian Girl Is "Ready For Marriage"', *Youth ki Awaaz*, 11 March 2014, https://www.youthkiawaaz.com/2014/03/patriarchy-dictates-indian-girl-ready-marriage/.
26. Suruchi Sharma, 'No country for single women', BBC, 4 March 2014, https://www.bbc.com/news/magazine-26341350.
27. '"You're too smart," and other jibes about being single', BBC, 14 March 2014, https://www.bbc.com/news/magazine-26578126.
28. Rana Dasgupta, *Capital: A Portrait of Twenty-First Century Delhi*, Fourth Estate, 2014.
29. Ritu Bhatia, 'Now, women are happy to stay single', *India Today*, 23 December 2011, http://indiatoday.intoday.in/story/women-are-happy-to-stay-single/1/165579.html.
30. https://palashivf.com/2017/02/21/ivf-treatment-market-india/.
31. https://economictimes.indiatimes.com/news/politics-and-

nation/govt-introduces-bill-to-ban-commercial-surrogacy/articleshow/70227304.cms

32. Digant Raj Kapoor, '"Can You Afford Your Wife's Expenses?": Indian Society's Frustrating Idea Of A Good Husband', *Youth ki Awaaz*, March 2014, https://www.youthkiawaaz.com/2014/03/pressure-marriage-indian-men-never-discussed/.
33. Apoorva Dutt, 'How and why number of young Indian couples getting divorced has risen sharply', *Hindustan Times*, 4 January 2015, https://www.hindustantimes.com/sex-and-relationships/how-and-why-number-of-young-indian-couples-getting-divorced-has-risen-sharply/story-mEuaEoviW40d6slLZbGu6J.html.
34. Ruth Vanita, 'Same-Sex Weddings, Hindu Traditions and Modern India', *Feminist Review*, February 2009.
35. Pamposh Raina, 'For Indian Women, Divorce is a Raw Deal', *The New York Times India Ink*, 22 March 2012, http://india.blogs.nytimes.com/2012/03/22/for-indian-women-divorce-a-raw-deal/?_r=0.
36. Amit Varma, 'We Should Celebrate Rising Divorce Rates', *India Uncut*, 19 May 2008, https://indiauncut.com/we-should-celebrate-rising-divorce-rates/.
37. Damayanti Datta, 'Confessions', *India Today*, 14 March 2017, https://www.indiatoday.in/magazine/sex-survey/story/20170320-sex-confessions-men-women-india-today-sex-survey-985955-2017-03-14.
38. 'Section 377: Here is everything you need to know', *The Economic Times*, 7 September 2018, https://economictimes.indiatimes.com/news/politics-and-nation/sc-delivers-historic-verdict-heres-everything-you-need-to-know-about-section-377/articleshow/65698429.cms.
39. http://www.sxpolitics.org/wp-content/uploads/2009/03/article-douglas-sanders.pdf
40. https://factly.in/tracing-the-history-of-ipc-section-377/
41. Dean Nelson, 'Hindu guru claims homosexuality can be "cured" by yoga', *The Telegraph*, 8 July 2009,

https://www.telegraph.co.uk/news/worldnews/asia/india/5780028/Hindu-guru-claims-homosexuality-can-be-cured-by-yoga.html.

42. Jiddu Krishnamurti, 'On homosexuality', YouTube, 8 December 2018, https://www.youtube.com/watch?v=ORNCfV1YyRE&t=182s.
43. Sudhir Kakar and Katharina Kakar, *The Indians: Portrait of a People*, Penguin, 2007.
44. Shara Ashraf, 'Parents forcing gay sons into marriage is criminal: LGBT activists', *Hindustan Times*, 22 April 2015, https://www.hindustantimes.com/sex-and-relationships/parents-forcing-gay-sons-into-marriage-is-criminal-lgbt-activists/story-CumVB79u6htEd2Mzfwum8I.html.
45. Ashok Row Kavi, 'Married Gay Men and their social implications,' http://www.ndtv.com/convergence/ndtv/new/ndtv-show-special-story.aspx?ID=275.
46. https://www.theweek.in/columns/guest-columns/2018/09/28/marriage-proposal.html
47. Jill Reynolds, *The Single Woman: A Discursive Investigation*, Routledge, 2008.
48. Eric Klinenberg, *Going Solo: The Extraordinary Rise and Surprising Appeal of Living Alone*, Penguin Books, 2013.
49. There are 71.4 million single women, or 12 per cent of the female population.

    There was a 39 per cent increase in the number of single women in India, the numbers rising from 51.2 million in 2001 to 71.4 million in 2011, according to census data. This includes widows, divorcees and unmarried women, and those deserted by husbands.
50. https://www.thehindu.com/society/is-single-the-new-black-for-indian-women-its-complicated/article22529203.ece.
51. https://www.indiaspend.com/as-indian-women-leave-jobs-single-women-keep-working-heres-why-71758/.
52. https://economictimes.indiatimes.com/magazines/panache/

lifestyle/there-is-a-big-misconception-that-single-women-arent-contented-journalist-kalpana-sharma/articleshow/70308582.cms.

53. https://www.indiaspend.com/as-indian-women-leave-jobs-single-women-keep-working-heres-why-71758/.
54. https://www.gqindia.com/content/single-male-indian-disease.

ACKNOWLEDGEMENTS

The contents of this book have in many ways been stimulated by the conversations, the discussions, the presentations, the arguments, the struggle, the focus and the continuum of the forum, Women Work & Health and its many members, some very dear to me. Though this cannot be an exhaustive list, I mention a few names with special gratitude: Hanna Westberg, Carina Hellgren, Annika Härenstam and Birgitta Jordansson from Sweden; Surinder Jaswal, Vibhuti Patel and Christine Nathan from Mumbai; Caroline Mangan from Ireland and Liisa Piitulainen Numminen from Finland.

Sunita Kaistha is a part of this group and more – my friend and partner in our various interventions in the world of gender and work.

To the women and girls of Sangam Vihar, Delhi and specially those connected to the WWHI Community Educational Centre, with a special shoutout to its supervisor Kanti Srivastava – this book is inspired by your often unspoken stories.

Amppe (Anna-Kaisa Heikkinen) – kittos, dear dost, through you so many worlds have opened including that of languages.

Teesta Guha Sarkar, my fabulous editor to whom I owe a

special thank you for endowing this book with its own idiom and rhythm. Thank you to Shradha, I couldn't have asked for a more meticulous copy editor.

Namita Gokhale with whom the seeds of friendship sown in my early years in Delhi, continue to be nourished and cherished, thank you too for your insights. Sanjoy Roy for just being the person you are and your support as an emphatic champion of the gender world. Lakshmi Kannan, for your wit and that abiding memory of a shared joke. Navtej Sarna for your reading of the chapters of this book. Ravi Veloor for reading the initial drafts. and Pavan K. Verma for discussions beyond *sanatan dharma*.

To my family, I don't have the words to express my deepest gratitude for your love, support, for simply being there and being a lodestar. Pitaji, my father, for directing a fledgling interest in reading to fanning the flame. Rajiv, my spouse and my children, Divya, Chaitanya, Abhinav and Priya for embracing me and my ways, and the darlings – Annaira and Aarav. I thank other members of my family amongst the Sahayas and Nigams (an extra-special hug for my niece Akshita for giving the necessary data for the millennial view) and Vermas in Jhansi for being there always. To Chachi (Shashi) for your stories about women from the earlier eras. For making me understand the world of weddings better – Vivekji and Reenaji, Arun and Asha.

For inputs that have been part of this journey of learning: Sangeeta Sahaya Prasad, Manjusha Maheshwari, Ashok Prasad, Aseem Srivastava and Smita Luther.

For the many contributors who helped in adding to the surveys, and to those who shared their professional knowledge: Kajal Srivastava in Bengaluru who cajoled and pursued her friends to fill the survey forms; Ratna Chaddha for your insights into high-end weddings, Dr Yuvakshi Juneja for medical insights. Ankit

Malhotra for sharing the madness of wedding planning; Upasana Agarwal, founder Amra Odbhut in Kolkata and to the millennials: Shivani and Pritish.

To the Mast Mastani group, for your joie de vivre and support. The Full Circle Group, a continuing script of friendship and fun. Friends in Delhi, Kolkata, Chennai and other parts of the world, your love stays with me.

This journey is tucked amongst the leaves of childhood memories – of rooms lined with bookshelves – curious tomes filling their spaces, well thumbed editions that belonged to my great grandfather, the eminent Hindi writer Vrindavanlal Varma. To him I am indebted for making writing a sacred vocation and to whom I owe the privilege of translating his classic, *Jhansi ki Rani: Lakshmibai*. And to Babu (Satyadev Varma), for literary and spiritual musings through childhood years.